house

American Houses for the New Century

Cathy Lang Ho and Raul A. Barreneche

UNIVERSE

To my loving family. —CLH

To my family and to Jean-Pierre, for their love and support. —RAB

First published in the United States of America in 2001 by UNIVERSE PUBLISHING
A Division of Rizzoli International Publications, Inc.,
300 Park Avenue South, New York, NY 10010

01 02 03 04 05 / 10 9 8 7 6 5 4 3 2 1

Editor: Terence Maikels
Book Design: Claudia Brandenburg
Front and back cover photos: Palmer/Rose house by Rick Joy © Wayne Fuji

Manufactured in China

Introduction:
American Houses
For the New Century
Cathy Lang Ho

The idea and function, image and reality of the house vary from culture to culture, locale to locale, generation to generation, demographic to demographic. Houses do much more than provide a roof over our heads: They are sanctuaries, havens—our private kingdoms, our personalized cocoons. They are the backdrops to our everyday lives. They are inheritances, tying us to the past, or investments, ensuring our future. They are status symbols. They are a neighborhood's building blocks, with the potential to build—or kill—a sense of community. They are economic indicators. They are expositions on culture, society, and technology. For architects, they are dream jobs, test beds, manifestos.

So vast and variable are the interpretations of this most fundamental building type that it is perhaps natural that it became the symbol of the American dream—the dream of creating one's safe, perosnal place in the world. This book presents examples that illuminate the changing ideas and ideals that shape the contemporary house in North America. (We include works by Canadians Brigitte Shim, Howard Sutcliffe, and Brian MacKay-Lyons and Mexican Alberto Kalach, not only to convey a broader—and more accurate—sense of the word

"American," but because their houses result from sensibilities and processes they share with their colleagues in the neighboring United States.) The objective of *House* is to present specimens that actively engage the questions of how houses are built, how they are rooted (and root us) to their locales, and how we use and regard them.

The first section, "Tectonics," features buildings that push materials and building techniques to new expressions or in new contexts, continuing the modernist quest for the progressive application of ever-evolving technology. Next, "Context" showcases houses that actively engage their sites. In the critical regionalist tradition, they employ materials, techniques, and forms that deepen the meaning of architecture in its particular context—an approach of increasing consequence as globalism renders the world ever more homogenous, and as cultural and environmental sustainability becomes acknowledged as not just a priority but a necessity. Lastly, "Revolutions" addresses the significant shifts our lifestyles have undergone, and how the house has responded to them. We are not so much suggesting that the architecture in this chapter is revolutionary, as much as we are

saying that it creatively responds to the rapidly changing demands, functions, and conceptions of the contemporary house.

We must admit that we were self-conscious about subtitling the book "American Houses for the New Century," which has a visionary ring to it. While we strongly believe that the houses in this book are among the best residential designs in North America at the turn of the twenty-first century, we are also aware that they likely will not survive the century without being modified, or even demolished, to make way for other constructions more appropriate to the changing times. Visionary projects, in any case, seldom retain a sense of timelessness, from Frank Lloyd Wright's low-cost Usonian Houses to Buckminster Fuller's Dymaxion House to various experimental Houses of Tomorrow. Even the landmark Case Study houses, sponsored by *Arts and Architecture* magazine from 1945 to 1969, are timepieces of sorts. These experiments did, however, introduce important ideas to the realm of domestic architecture, from socially liberating open plans to cost-efficient methods of prefabrication—ideas that have continued to influence house designs to this day.

The postwar housing development Levittown, in Long Island, New York, made the American Dream—owning a detached, single-family house in the suburbs—accessible to many. With mortgage subsidies and tax deductions, these modest houses were designed for the working male and his dependent wife and children. Although the nuclear family has long since given way to a variety of nontraditional family configurations, this house type persists as the model for mass house production, creating many of the housing and urban problems we face today. (Bernard Hoffman, *Life* magazine, ©1950, Time, Inc.)

In 1998, New York-based architect Michael Bell organized the exhibition *16 Houses* to address the housing problems of Houston's poorest neighborhood, the Fifth Ward. The predominantly black residents' housing options are restricted to, mainly, dilapidated shotgun shacks. Bell invited sixteen prominent architects to design houses, buildable at under $75,000, to demonstrate that affordable housing need not sacrifice good design. Bell worked with the Fifth Ward Community Redevelopment Corporation (CRC), which has helped to translate federal housing assistance into down-payment vouchers for households at below-median incomes. The CRC and representatives from the community selected six of the houses, including Bell's own design **(above)**, to be built.

Bell's design, dubbed Glass House No. 347 @ 2 Degrees, is the latest interpretation of the famed glass houses that turned modern architecture on its head. His refined glass pavilion uses primarily off-the-shelf materials, in the tradition of the postwar Case Study houses. Winner of a prestigious Progressive Architecture Award in 2001 (and published in the April issue of *Architecture* magazine), Bell's project inspired jurors to debate at how its design—though not especially novel in a formal sense, and essentially a revival of 1950s modernism—remains revolutionary in its context. It demonstrates that modern design still has a long way to go before penetrating the stronghold that traditional house imagery and construction have on mass house-building.

The houses in this book, similarly, offer valuable lessons on how to construct the house, physically and psychologically. For example, many of them reinterpret and recontextualize materials and concepts from other realms of life. Several of the architects in this book turn to industrial materials, inspired by their ruggedness, economy, and prosaic qualities. Anne Fougeron was drawn to channel glass; Alberto Kalach felt liberated by reinforced concrete; and heavy-duty metal sparked the imaginations of Brian MacKay-Lyons; Daly, Genik; Miller/Hull; Rick Joy; and Barton Myers. Many houses have also borrowed spatial ideas from other building types, domesticating elements from the office, museum galleries, and art studios. Even if the houses in this book—like all custom, architect-designed houses—are singular (and expensive), their architects, like generations before them, are using the territory of the small-scale, domestic building to explore methods and concepts of building that may be further explicated in their own or others' future work.

Finding these houses, we must say, was not as easy as we thought it would be. We expected to find many more projects that challenge what house-building and house-dwelling is all about—that take into consideration the varied and sophisticated materials and processes we now have (or should have) at our disposal, the new attitudes we have about the relationship between building and the environment, and the fast-changing patterns of our daily lives. Instead, the majority of the houses built at the dawn of the twenty-first century are still mostly wood stud, sheetrock, and stucco, appearing in a sprawl of unending suburbs and following much the same template that served the average household—white, middle-class family with male head of household, housewife, and three kids—of more than half a century ago. Postwar developments like Levittown in Long Island, New York, provided the formula for mass-produced, detached, single-family suburban houses that continues to be the basis of mass house production today.

In the important classic *Redesigning the American Dream: The Future of Housing, Work, and Family Life* (Norton, 1984), author Dolores Hayden observes that the adoption of Levittown as a model for housing in the United States "is at the heart of the housing problem" the country has experienced ever since. Despite the fact that households have

New York–based Sulan Kolatan and William MacDonald are among the leading protagonists in digital architecture. They are pushing the architectural applications of CNC (computer numerically controlled) technology, to enable complex designs to move from 3D digital models to physical building components. The frame of their bloblike addition to the Raybould House in Connecticut is formed by irregularly shaped, milled plywood ribs. This technique is at the heart of "mass customization"—the mass production of unique forms.

been getting smaller over the decades, the production of most housing in the United States and the financing structure that perpetuates it (e.g., bank loans and tax subsidies) continue to favor this stagnant domestic form.

Hayden further observes, "Single people, male or female, old or young, straight or gay, often find that the housing options available to them lack flexibility, variety, and complexity." How often do we hear of divorced individuals unable to make their mortgage payments, or empty-nesters whose houses no longer suit them? In our book, we included several multigenerational houses (Steven Holl's Y House; Toshiko Mori's Cohen House; Daly, Genik's Valley Center House), adaptations of old house types (Public's Su Mei Yu House, Wesley Wei's Pennsylvania House), and rehabilitations of nondomestic building types (RoTO's Carlson-Reges House) to underscore the idea that, just as demographics and lifestyles have undergone a radical reconfiguration, so must the house. The most pressing point to make about housing today, ultimately, is the need for more choices.

The projects in this book are united by their attempts to push the house in new directions. It is worth mentioning their kinship with the work of several architects who are also producing noteworthy alternatives, even if their ideas have not yet been realized in built form. New York architect Michael Bell recently organized *16 Houses*, an exhibition that invited sixteen prominent architects to design affordable houses for one of Houston's poorest neighborhoods, the predominantly black Fifth Ward. Bell worked with the nonprofit Fifth Ward Community Redevelopment Corporation, which translated federal housing assistance into downpayment vouchers, shifting aid from large-scale rental projects to single-family homeownership. Bell's Glass House No. 347 @ 2 Degrees, a refined glass pavilion using mostly off-the-shelf components, demonstrates—like many others in the exhibition—that high design need not be the sole terrain of the affluent. Six of the houses (including Bell's) were chosen by the local community to be built, and buyers are already lined up.

It is important to note that the lack of affordable housing is hurting not only the poor but the gainfully employed middle class, who were especially squeezed by skyrocketing land and real estate prices at the end of the 1990s. Realizing that part of the problem is the stronghold that slow-moving and unimaginative builders and bankers

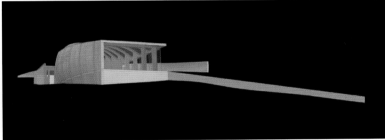

The landform of Montana architect William Massie's own house, set on the rolling hills of Meagher County, traces the topography of the site. The Big Belt House's undulating form, derived from mapping data produced by global positioning devices, would not have been achievable without CNC processes. With the aid of software, the architect calculated the dimensions and weight-loads of a series of arching, cross-sectional frames that, once in place, resemble a ribcage. The frames are made of concrete, poured into uniquely milled molds.

More than 1,500 pieces of rigid foam were machined into parts for the molds, which were assembled on site like a puzzle. Once in place, concrete was poured into the molds, to form the ribcage-like frame. The frame was then wrapped in PVC pipes, which gave the exterior its curving surface. The PVC substrate (which creates airspace and insulation) was sprayed with Shotcrete (a light spray-on concrete), resulting in a new expression of thin-shelled construction, akin to the explorations of Eero Saarinen and Pier Luigi Nervi.

have over the bulk of production housing, architects like New York–based Kolatan/MacDonald Studio and William Massie in Montana are investigating ways to bypass some of the intermediary steps between design and construction. For the Raybould House in Fairfield County, Connecticut (in its test phase in early 2001), Sulan Kolatan and William MacDonald are employing CNC (computer numerically controlled) technology to translate three-dimensional computer renderings directly to physical components, which can be sculpted from anything from dense foam to resin to wood. In theory, an entire house can be milled and produced in a matter of weeks. Similarly, Massie is milling molds with which to form his house's poured-in-place concrete frame. Without the computer, he would not have been able to create (barring exorbitant expense) the undulating landform of his Big Belt House, now under construction in the rolling hills of Montana, for each mold is unique and fits together like a jigsaw puzzle. The historic premise of cheap building has been the standardization of parts and assembly processes, which exploited economies of scale, but also led to dull, repetitive, identical results. Both Kolatan/MacDonald and Massie are pioneers

in developing an approach that can revolutionize the housing industry—"mass-produced customization," which can yield unique environments at no more time or expense as it would take to produce identical ones.

Houston-based Mark Wamble and Dawn Finley of Interloop Architects also tackle the question of mass production with the KLIP Binder House, which they developed for the *16 Houses* exhibition. A theoretical project, it is a system of modular house sections that can be bought individually and clipped together to expand or shrink the house as necessary. The architects welcome the influence of consumer products manufacturing and branding, and without cynicism, suggest it would be possible to have production costs offset by selling advertising space on individual clip units. "Why not treat house parts as we do our stereos? Why shouldn't we be able to trade them in constantly for the new top-of-the-line models? And who can deny that a house should perform as well as a car?" Wamble asks. The KLIP House plays into our consumer society, while harkening to prefab principles of the sort advanced by Fuller in the Dymaxion House and the Case Study architects. It also recalls the corporate sponsorship of building

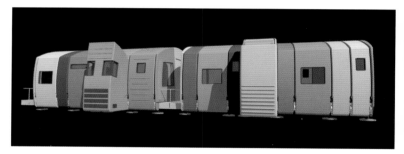

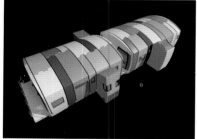

Though the premise of the *16 Houses* exhibition in Houston was to produce buildable designs to which federally subsidized down-payment vouchers could be applied, local architects Mark Wamble and Dawn Finley tackled the larger questions of the economics of house production. Speculating on what would be possible if a handful of vouchers were invested in a production technique rather than the production of a single house, they developed the KLIP Binder House, a prototype for a building system. Taking cues from consumer products manufacturing, the KLIP Binder House is composed of modular injection-molded components, with unique functions, features, personalities, and even sponsors/manufacturers.

KLIP is the ultimate transformable house, which can respond immediately if someone moves in or out without notice, if an unexpected pregnancy occurs, if an elderly relative suddenly needs boarding, and so on. Wamble and Finley propose that the KLIPs be regarded as consumer products, akin to stereo components, which competing manufacturers produce, market, and continually improve. Logos or brand names could appear on the surfaces, just as they appear on other objects in our everyday life.

research, which materials manufacturers such as Reynolds Aluminum and Monsanto Plastics underwrote a half century ago.

While some are busy revolutionizing the production of housing, others are intent on improving the house's daily workings. Most provocative is MIT's House_N, an $11 million research project devoted to the development of a "Smart House," which is not so much a specific design as a system that transforms the house into a responsive machine that can be tailored to homeowners' particular needs. House_N researchers are now testing walls imbedded with sensors that can monitor energy consumption, climate, safety conditions, and even the health of its occupants. Microsoft, too, has gotten in on the act, hiring architects to work with its programmers to design its version of the House of the Future. The software giant is researching ways of rigging home appliances with Internet access and networking all of them. Already, car stereos are equipped for getting maps, weather reports, and traffic updates. Consumer electronics researchers believe that soon all electronic products will have Internet capability. Ultimately, it will be possible to activate, either by voice or remote control, a house's lights, music, TVs, VCRs, security

systems, window blinds, everything. MIT, Microsoft, as well as IBM and Sony, which are conducting similar research, are pushing toward the creation of houses that homeowners can communicate with, and vice versa.

In this experimental vein is New York architect Michael McDonough's eHouse2000, which focuses particularly on "smart"—*e.g.*, energy-efficient, high-performance, environmentally minded—materials. With sponsorship from large corporations that donated their products, the eHouse (under construction in Ulster County, New York) has such features as electricity-producing photovoltaic panels, self-healing zinc and tin-coated stainless steel roofing, CNC-cut structural insulated panels, and a hydroponic garden that will oxygenate the air.

We mention these examples to press the point that the following houses are part of an ongoing tradition, a step forward from the past, offering a promising vision of the future. Residential architecture has always been utopian, envisioning a better way to live and build, for the creation of a more efficient, equitable, healthy, leisurely society, and now, as well, a cleaner, safer world. This is the tradition that the projects in *House* uphold.

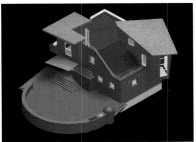

Pooling resources from MIT's School of Architecture and Planning, Media Lab, and other technology departments, House_N is a broad research project devoted to the development of the latest house of tomorrow— the Smart House. Under the direction of professors Kent Larson and Chris Luebkeman, the project is an open experiment that tests the feasibility of such things as robotic equipment, photovoltaic-lined walls that create and store energy, transformable spaces, and networked appliances that can communicate information to residents on everything from the temperature inside to the status of groceries. Wireless sensors worn by occupants allow the house to monitor their health, nutrition, and exercise.

New York architect Michael McDonough rightly believes that true architectural innovation must lead to environmental benefits. His eHouse2000 is a testing ground for green building products, developed in conjunction with large manufacturers that donated their materials. Among its features are a wooden truss system made of unused low-end lumber, flooring made of sustainable bamboo, a hydroelectric power system, and walls with computer chips that monitor air quality, energy consumption, and the status of the radiant cooling and heating systems.

Tectonics

If you had asked the average American forty years ago how he or she imagined living in 2001, their domestic vision of the future would surely have involved zipping home in Jetsons-style spaceships. After all, the 1960s were the dawn of the space age, and thoughts of a brave new day-to-day life made possible by futuristic technology gripped the popular imagination. Rocket missions had everyone thinking they would soon be living on the moon—or at least in some futuristic earthbound home worthy of NASA.

In reality, life at the beginning of the twenty-first century has been far from space-aged, and the residential design industry, perhaps more than other segments of our high-tech economy, could hardly be called futuristic. In fact, much of the home design world seems downright archaic given the technological advances that have changed just about every other aspect of our lives. The fact is most people live in relatively old-fashioned houses made of the same materials—wood, brick, stone—that architects have been designing with for centuries. Even homes made of steel, first pioneered by the modernists of the early twentieth century, have barely evolved since the industrial metal was first tried out on the home front. Architect Kent Larsen, who is heading a promising research mission into the home of the future at MIT, finds the materials we used to build houses as antiquated as the ways we build them. Larsen makes a poignant commentary on the state of affairs when he says that we are still building homes by hand, just as cars were manufactured in the earliest days of the now highly automated auto industry.

American architects' attitudes toward materials in the last century have changed greatly, to say the least. The century started out on a high note for splendid materials and elaborate craft, with strong influence from the work of architects abroad: Arts and Crafts mastermind William Morris in England, Victor Horta in Belgium, and Charles Rennie Mackintosh in Scotland. Americans such as Louis Sullivan and Frank Lloyd Wright in Chicago and Greene & Greene in California had different agendas behind the houses they designed, but they all looked to rich, home-grown materials to further their ideas about the American home.

The 1920s gave birth to architecture's machine age. Suddenly, tried and tested materials went out the window and were replaced by hard-nosed industrial elements of glass, steel, and aluminum, which was used for the first time in houses instead of factories and airplanes. The United States became home to die-hard European-born modernists like Ludwig Mies van der Rohe and Walter Gropius, who both fled World War II–era Germany, and fostered its own breed of homespun modernists, among them Charles and Ray Eames and Philip Johnson. Le Corbusier passionately preached the idea of homes as "machines for living," and the manifestation of this concept proliferated well into the 1970s, with the notable exception of Frank Lloyd Wright's organic designs.

The rise of postmodernism and the revival of classicism killed the drive to explore materials. The work of architects like

Miami's Arquitectonica made a mockery out of material culture. Instead of substantive natural elements like stone, wood, or concrete—or even sleek high-tech materials—they used thin veneers of cheap stucco to distinguish their flashy buildings. Designers that turned to the past for inspiration, including Robert A. M. Stern, Michael Graves, and the rehabilitated modernist Johnson, also turned their backs on real materials in favor of thin classical imagery. In the golden age of the real classics, Corinthian columns were made of solid stone; in the 1980s, they were made of hollow fiberglass.

The 1990s saw the gradual demise of postmodernism and classical impulses, and a thriving rebirth of modernism, in both spirit and style. There has been a new craze for the modernist classics, especially the steel-and-glass houses of early modernists like Richard Neutra and Albert Frey. But this modernist renaissance gave rise to a new generation of architects concerned with pushing the boundaries of materials. Some are looking to employ entirely new materials in their domestic designs, or finding new ways of using old elements. Tucson architect Rick Joy, for instance, is creating seemingly revolutionary houses out of rammed earth. It is actually an old way of building in the desert of the American Southwest, but Joy has refined its construction to the point where it is as polished and sophisticated as the most pristine concrete. Similarly, Joy is using rusty steel wrappers to enclose houses he has designed in the Arizona desert. It is also an antiquated material, but still relatively unused in residential design, especially at such a large scale and with such great finesse.

San Francisco architect Anne Fougeron looked to a staple of European industrial buildings, channels made of laminated glass, to create a crystalline stair tower in a sophisticated house in Palo Alto. And Barton Myers, in a move seemingly inspired by the artist Marcel Duchamp, created a home for himself from off-the-shelf industrial components such as steel roofs and roll-up garage doors. In all of these examples, the materials themselves are not newly invented; the designers simply use them in inventive ways to solve pressing problems. In this sense, these architects are continuing the spirit of invention and innovation created by the early modernists. But their attention to materials also conveys a sensual, expressive quality well beyond functional issues, something with which the early modernists would surely have taken issue. Look at the luminous precision of Fougeron's channel-glass stair tower or the raw power of Joy's rusty, Richard Serra–inspired steel boxes. These material choices are pragmatic—but also poetic.

Some contemporary architects, though avowed modernists, turn to tried-and-true materials and craft them with razor sharp precision to carry out modern design ideas. Toronto architects Brigitte Shim and Howard Sutcliffe, for instance, designed a tiny boathouse in rural Ontario that displays an exceptional level of craftsmanship in the many kinds of wood used throughout the house. It is undoubtedly a modern house, but its exacting craft and some old-fashioned flourishes—inspired by rustic, century-old cottages in that part of Canada—seem a throwback to another age. They even borrowed the almost primitive (but functional) local construction technique of building on foundations of stone-filled wood crates, submerged into the lake. In Mexico City, Alberto Kalach designed a serene home made entirely of concrete. There is nothing revolutionary about its construction; its precise craftsmanship, though, helps make its simple, moody spaces all the more powerful and crisply contemporary.

What could be considered a revolutionary change in domestic design is the clients' desire to surround themselves with materials once deemed purely industrial, and with exposed structure. Even the owners of expensive, highly refined homes have no shame in living with uncovered wooden beams and raw concrete floors; in fact, such hearty industrial elements are an important part of the image of their dwellings. While it is possible that these clients have been won over by the modernist impulses of their architects, a far more likely culprit is the enduring fashion of urban lofts. Ironically, lofts developed their signature style out of necessity, as artists in New York and other large cities began adapting former factory floors into cheap residential spaces and could not afford to cover up their cast-iron columns and beams and exposed plumbing. Thirty years later, that look has become highly valued; the privilege of living with hanging pipes and open roof joists in converted factories can now cost more than a million dollars. Of course, along with the material esthetic of lofts comes the functional benefit of wide-open, flexible spaces instead of confined rooms housing a single function. As so many of the houses in this book reveal, even the clients of new homes want a piece of the loft lifestyle, in terms of both form and function.

Domestic design at the beginning of the twenty-first century may fall far short of the futuristic expectations of the twentieth century, and the home building industry may seem lethargic compared to the rest of our fast-paced society, but the modern spirit of investigation into materials is once again alive and well. This time, it is not only about discovering the new, but also finding ways of transforming time-honored materials into powerful new expressions.

Fougeron Architecture
440 House
Palo Alto, California
2000

Located in the heart of the Silicon Valley, Palo Alto is one of the Bay Area's oldest and most charming suburbs—not to mention real-estate poor. The high-tech explosion has driven property values to extremes that hardly correlate to Palo Alto's large stock of modest suburban homes. As neighborhoods struggle to stave off "mansionization," new residents find themselves living in overpriced tract houses. The challenge for San Francisco–based architect Anne Fougeron was to create a modern house worthy of its hefty price tag, while working within the constraining context of banal ranchburgers.

Fougeron's clients, a successful professional couple with no children, wanted a luxury home. They owned a one-story standard ranch house on a constricted lot, which the architect managed to usher through city planning as a remodel by staying within the footprint of the old house. An entirely new, utterly modern, sleek two-story, 5,000-square-foot house materialized in its place.

The luxurious and modern feel of the house derives from its rich materials and pure geometry. An articulated box, the house's rooms are organized around a double-height glazed living room, at the heart of the house. A polished black granite entry walk leads into this grand space, which is flanked by two semi-symmetrical volumes of glass and French limestone. They contain, on the ground floor, a guestroom and office in one wing, and the kitchen/family room in the other. The transparency of the façade—one can see straight through the house's glazed midsection to the back garden—is balanced by the dignified limestone that anchors the house's corners and gives it an air of monumentality. The polished granite of the entry walk is carried through the living room and spills to the rear terrace, contributing to the house's fluidity of space.

This sense of spatial continuity is deepened by another feature, a circulation spine containing the staircase and hallway, which penetrates the house from front to back. It becomes a continuous object as a result of its unique material treatment. Fougeron liked the idea of load-bearing channel glass, commonly used in European industrial buildings, because it is suitable as outdoor cladding, and beautiful enough to be used indoors. The refined recontextualization of this type of glass in a dwelling is itself a form of material invention.

To adapt an industrial material like channel glass to a domestic context requires innovative detailing. The architect overlapped the glass channels to create a double-walled glass construction with added depth and a higher insulating value. Its milky surface quality brings a soft light into the object and its adjacent spaces. For an added layer of visual shielding and geometric composition, the architect wrapped the stairwell (which projects from the front façade) in a woven steel cage. At night, the entire volume glows like a lantern, and the shadows of its inhabitants' movement are played against its surface, confounding the typical thresholds that homeowners have for privacy.

The glass house in architectural history has signified great technological, ideological, and psychological leaps. The capability of glass to become more than a filter of light and air—to become structural and, recently, power-saving and power-producing (rigged with solar energy cells)—has ushered it into new realms of building. The more glass, one might say, the more modern the architecture (and this is especially true for houses, where its application can be considered more risqué). Though an utterly reductive statement, the landmarks of modern architecture seem to support it. Pierre Chareau's Maison de Verre, Philip Johnson's house in New Canaan, Mies van der Rohe's Farnsworth House, and many works that appeared in the 1998 Museum of Modern Art exhibition *The Unprivate House*, illustrate the degree to which glass houses are, at the dawn of the twenty-first century, an ongoing experiment.

Flanking the front entrance is the stairwell, which is entirely encased in load–bearing channel glass, commonly used in European industrial buildings. The architect liked the material because it is rugged enough to be used as outdoor cladding and beautiful enough to appear indoors. The unique material treatment renders the stairwell a distinct object, resembling a lantern, displaying the shadows of its inhabitants on its milky surface. For an added level of privacy, each bay has an operable stainless steel mesh panel.

The double-height, glazed living room at the center of the house spills to the back terrace. The granite flooring is used continuously, from the front entrance path to the interior to the rear terrace, to accentuate a sense of flowing space. To the left of the living room is the kitchen/ family room on the ground floor and master bedroom above; to the right is an office with guest bedroom above.

15
house

Tectonics Fougeron Architecture, 440 House

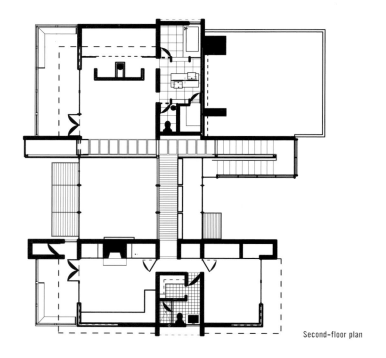

On the first floor **(below)**, the open living room at the house's center separates the kitchen/family room (attached to the street-facing garage) from the offices/guestroom wing. The second-floor plan **(above)** shows the master bedroom above the kitchen, linked to another guest bedroom and gym room by a bridge that overlooks the double-height living room.

Second-floor plan

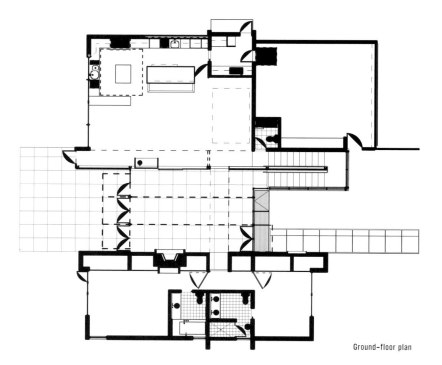

Ground-floor plan

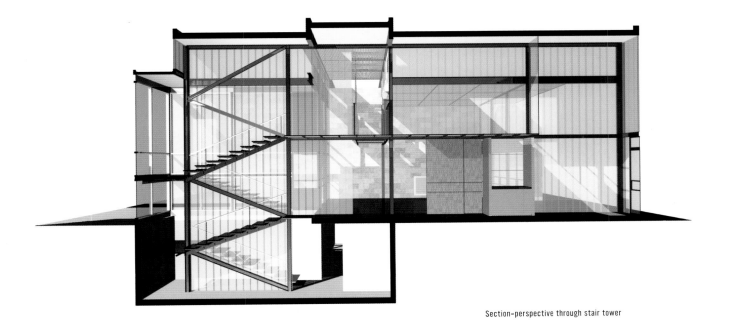

Section-perspective through stair tower

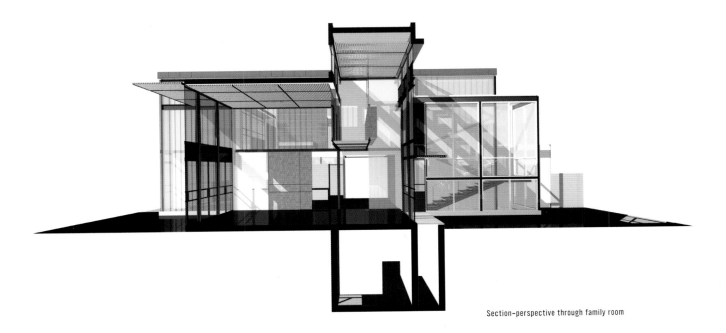

Section-perspective through family room

The channel-glass volume that projects from the front façade as the stairwell **(this page)** is continued as a circulation corridor that penetrates the house and extends to the rear garden **(facing page)**. A steel brise-soleil extends above the rear façade's custom glass curtain wall.

Tectonics Fougeron Architecture, 440 House

A limestone-wrapped fireplace separates the living room from the dining room/kitchen. The diaphonous channel-glass wall extends into the space from the stairwell, at front.

View toward the stairwell at the front of the house, with the living room and front entry to the right. The architect specified only extra smooth and sensual surfaces.

A glass bridge on the second-floor overlooks the spacious living room, contributing to the house's overall sense of airiness.

The channel-glass encased volume contains a glass walkway on the second level, linking the stairs to the master bedroom (above); view from the kitchen toward the glass-sheathed corridor that separates it from the living room (center); in the master bathroom, materials include white marble, Panama granite, woven metal, and glass (below). Facing page: A polished-granite entry walk leads into the living room, a soaring, airy space that opens to the front and back of the house. French limestone anchors the corners of the office/guestroom wing, at left.

Palmer-Rose House
Tucson, Arizona
1998

In the hands of Tucson architect Rick Joy, the most common material—desert soil—becomes an extraordinary building element. Joy, who trained first as a carpenter in Maine and later as a designer in the office of Phoenix architect Will Bruder, has perfected the art and technique of creating clean, modern buildings from thick walls of rammed earth. A conceptual cousin of adobe, this material is a traditional one in the Southwest desert. To produce the walls, a mix of soil and cement is poured into wooden forms and tamped down in layers (the "ramming" part of "rammed earth"). When the material hardens and the supporting formwork is removed, beautiful, earth-colored surfaces with textured ribbons caused by the layering of soil are exposed.

The Palmer-Rose House is one of the best examples of this rammed-earth technique that Joy has constructed. Located in suburban Tucson, several miles from the Santa Catalina Mountains, the house is composed of individual volumes set into a natural desert landscape. One smaller structure, wrapped in weathered steel, houses a garage, workshop, and guest bedroom. Across an unpaved entry court is the main house, which is composed of two connected wings made of rammed earth. One wing contains the entrance; an airy, loft-like living room; kitchen; and a large, open-air porch with sweeping views of the surrounding mountains. The other wing contains the master bedroom, den, and an alfresco spa, open to the elements. The feeling created by these separate but related structures is of a sophisticated encampment in the desert.

Though the massiveness of the thick earth walls might suggest a dark interior of tiny, carved rooms, the 2,800-square-foot house has quite the opposite character: It is full of light and wide-open spaces. The living room, for instance, is an airy fluid space crowned by a soaring butterfly roof sheathed in wooden planks, with an expansive wall of floor-to-ceiling glass that opens onto mountain vistas. A skylight along a wall containing a fireplace and several square niches highlights the beautifully irregular layers and textures of the rammed-earth surfaces. A long kitchen island flanking the dining area doubles as a buffet table for dinner parties—and the whole room extends onto the covered porch at the far end of the room, effectively expanding the space to the outdoors.

The feeling of openness and light continues throughout the more private living quarters, with another north-facing wall of floor-to-ceiling glass in the bedroom. In the bedroom, however, there are a series of smaller, square windows set into the thick earth wall that create the feeling of a more protected, sheltered room. The adjoining study is also protected by tiny openings in the thick exterior walls.

The house's furnishings are kept deliberately simple but bold. Classic modern pieces and strong primary colors contrast with the quiet earth tones of the house itself and reinforce the idea that despite its ancient desert undertones, the home is a thoroughly modern dwelling.

At night, the north-facing glass wall of the master bedroom opens up the room to full view, revealing a thoroughly modern home in the desert. The floor-to-ceiling glass wall, sheltered by a V-shaped butterfly roof, opens up to views of the Santa Catalina Mountains.

The Palmer-Rose House's low-lying volumes, built of rammed earth and weathered steel, nestles into its setting of cacti and desert shrubs (above). The entry to the house is through an informal courtyard between the living and bedroom wings (facing page). A giant metal scupper extends far beyond the rammed-earth wall of the den. The site plan (facing page, below) shows the garage (at left) separated from the main house by a land-scaped courtyard.

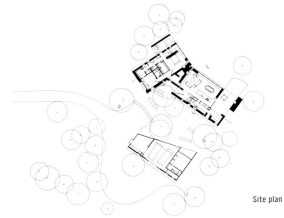

Site plan

A porch just off the kitchen (above) extends out into the desert garden. Large glass panes (at right) look back into the living room and dining room; the adjoining bedroom wing is visible in the background (at left). The covered portion of the terrace (facing page, above), creates a shaded outdoor dining terrace with a ceiling fan suspended from the wood-planked ceiling. A small fireplace is carved into the rammed-earth wall (at right).

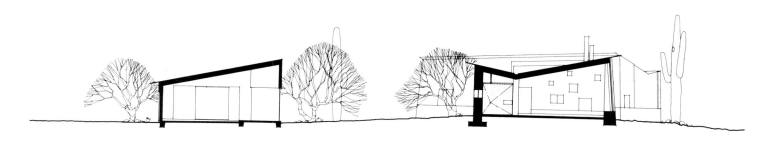

Site section

The front door
(this page) is a
hefty Douglas
fir portal that
pivots to create
the sensation
of a completely
open home. The
foyer opens
into the airy
kitchen and
dining room,
which is visible
through large
floor-to-
ceiling glass
walls and doors
that open onto a
shaded terrace
(facing page).

Tectonics Rick Joy Architect, Palmer-Rose House

A skylight along the main wall of the living room **(above)** casts sunlight and shadows on the irregular texture of the rammed-earth surface, which features square niches and a built-in fireplace. A chunky kitchen island overlooking the loftlike dining area contains the stove and sink, as well as dining stools for informal eating **(facing page, left)**. A glass door lets light into the kitchen **(facing page, right)** as well as breezes.

In the master bedroom **(above)**, sunlight casts strong patterns across the wooden wall enclosing a walk-in closet. In the entry foyer **(facing page)**, carefully placed skylights and windows create a moody wash of daylight on the layered, textured surfaces of the rammed-earth walls.

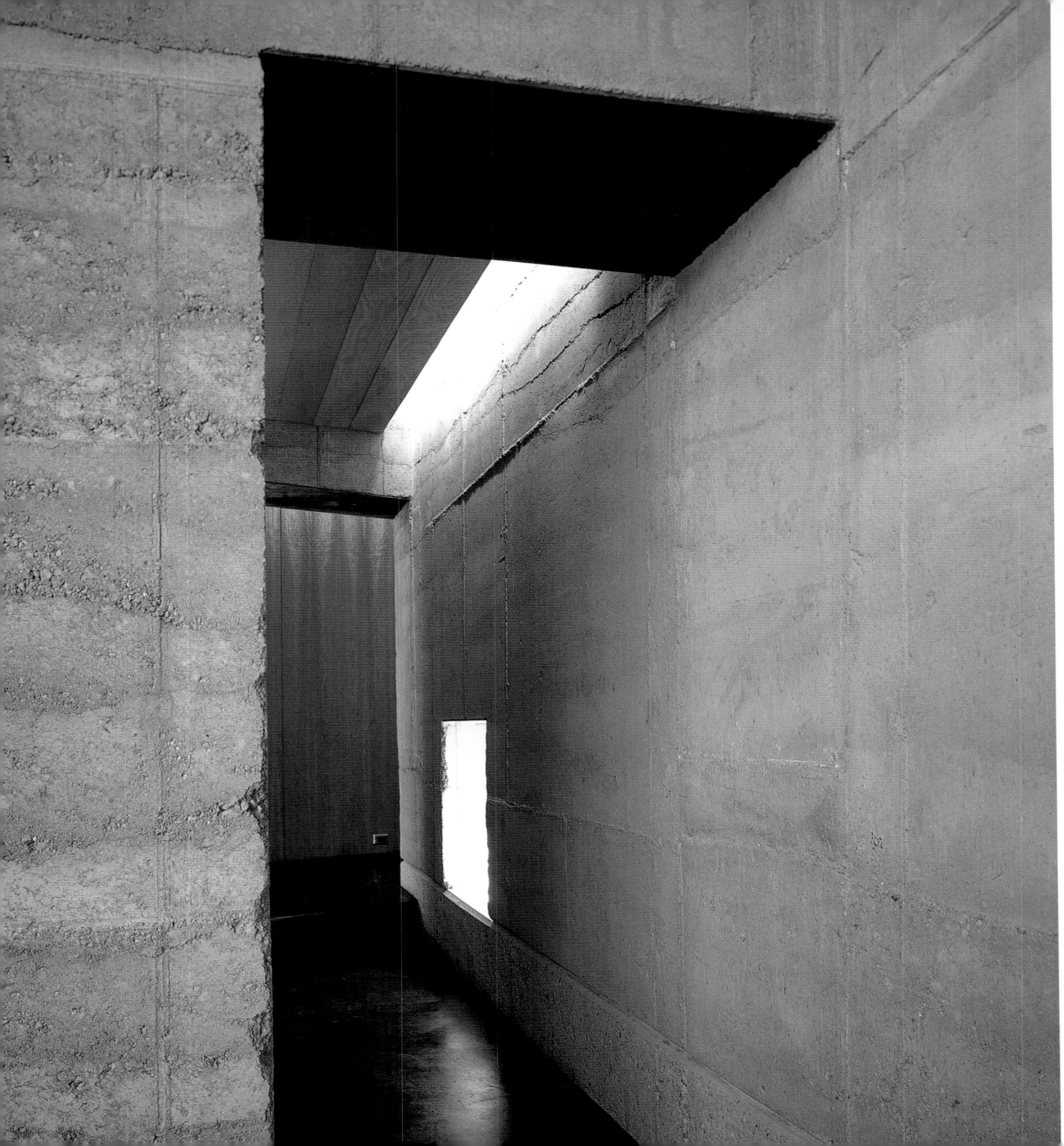

Shim+Sutcliffe Architects
Muskoka Boathouse
Lake Muskoka, Ontario, Canada
2000

Toronto architects Brigitte Shim and partner Howard Sutcliffe looked to a quirky yet time-tested local building technique to create a boathouse that literally rises out of the waters of Lake Muskoka, in the Canadian countryside north of Toronto. The foundations of the 2,300-square-foot structure are a series of wooden cribs filled with granite ballast. In wintertime, workers cut holes into the frozen water with chainsaws and dropped the empty wooden crates into the lake, filled them with granite chunks, and waited for the cribs to settle on the lakebed over the rest of the winter. In springtime, they began building the house atop the underwater foundations.

The boathouse is the latest addition to a lakeside vacation compound that comprises a large waterfront home and a 100-year-old cottage, where the home's owner entertains his family and business colleagues. The new boathouse contains a pair of indoor boatslips; storage areas for canoes, life jackets, and other boating equipment; a small bathroom with shower; and a tiny alfresco kitchen that opens onto the outdoor dock. Upstairs is a luxurious but simple living area, with a spacious master bedroom and sitting area; a compact kitchen tucked between the bedroom and a large bath and dressing area; and a covered porch overlooking the lake. There is also a small rooftop rock garden flanking the entrance to the second-floor living quarters, which gives the house a vaguely Japanese feeling.

The house is filled with nautical references, both in its overall imagery and detailing. For instance, the curving ceiling above the bedroom recalls the sleek, rounded profiles of boat hulls or the tarpaulins that cover docked ships, and the bands of horizontal windows overlooking Lake Muskoka recall the strips of windows on boats. As on a seagoing vessel, all of the furniture is built into the walls, including the bed, bookshelves, desks, and counters. (One benefit of so many built-in fixtures is that the compact living areas feel much larger.) The architects took advantage of every available square inch of space, squeezing storage space into walls and underneath counters.

Both inside and out, almost every surface of the house is made of wood, from the painted oak floors—a nod to the traditional rustic cabins of Lake Muskoka—to the custom mahogany cupboards, closets, and window frames, to the walls of birch plywood and light-colored Douglas fir. On the exterior of the house, the palette comprises painted, reclaimed timbers on the lakefront side, thin Douglas fir siding, planks of Jatoba wood (typically used as flooring but here installed as a wall), bands of mahogany window frames, and columns made from logs skewered on steel posts. By using so many different kinds of wood in so many combinations, the architects were able to tie the house into so many of its surroundings, from old-fashioned wooden boats to the area's rustic vacation cottages. The meticulous detailing and often unexpected treatment of the wood give an otherwise old-fashioned material a distinctly modern edge.

The boathouse—which comprises indoor and outdoor boatslips with a sleeping cabin above—is built on underwater foundations, so that it literally rises from the waters of Canada's Lake Muskoka. The exterior is clad in a variety of wood colors and textures, with a zinc-shingled roof.

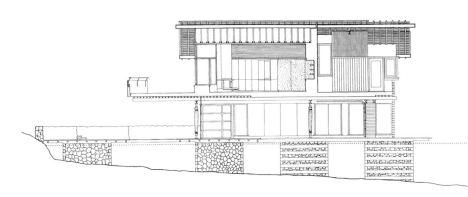

South elevation

East-west section

The boathouse's south elevation **(facing page, above)** faces an outdoor dock adjoining a wooden deck where the owners can entertain, thanks to a small outdoor kitchenette on the ground floor. The doors of the indoor boatslip are made of pearly, translucent fiberglass panels set into wooden garage-door frames **(facing page, below)**. A deck extending from the second-floor master bedroom and over the dock **(above, left and right)** overlooks the water. Another covered terrace extends from the bathroom at the other end of the house **(above, center)**. Sections through the boathouse **(above)** reveal foundations made of ballast-filled cribs submerged into the lake; the house rests directly on these underwater pilings.

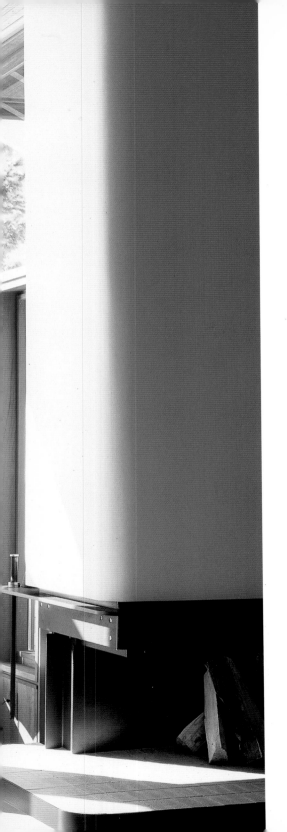

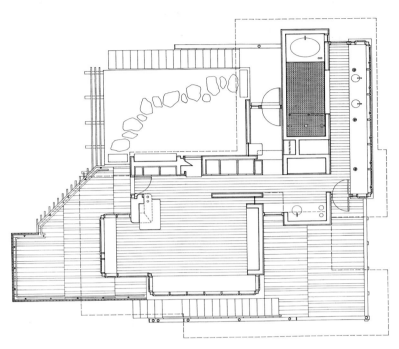

Ground-floor plan

The bedroom **(facing page)** boasts large expanses of windows overlooking a rooftop terrace and the woods beyond. The curving profiles of the wooden ceiling and plaster-covered fireplace, which was custom designed by the architects, recall the shapes of boat hulls and dockside tarpaulins.

The sleek master bedroom at the rear of the boat-house features Asian flourishes, including Japanese ceramic bowls used as wash basins **(above)** and a wood-enclosed soaking tub **(below)**. Mahogany-framed windows behind the sink overlook Lake Muskoka.

The master bedroom's curved ceiling and boat-like built-in furniture make the space feel bigger and give it a nautical character **(right)**. A built-in desk overlooking the lake **(at left)** and closets hidden behind mahogany panels **(at left)** provide extra storage. The floors are made of oak, painted a buttery yellow, as in the historic cottages of the area.

Rick Joy Architect
Tyler House
Tubac, Arizona
2001

Tucson architect Rick Joy has gained something of a reputation as "the rammed-earth guy," as he puts it, only half-jokingly (see Palmer-Rose House, page 24). The Tyler House, which he designed for a retired couple from Columbus, Ohio, marks the introduction of a new material for Joy: weathered steel. Though it may be a relatively new medium in the architect's work, it is by no means a first in the region. Metal buildings, which weather into rusty boxes if left unsealed, have evolved into a kind of rough-and-tumble vernacular since their humble beginnings as utility sheds and storage silos in the frontier days of the Southwest. Joy chose rusty metal as the main material for the Tyler House because of its obvious ties to the natural and manmade history of the region—and because its rough yet sophisticated quality has a powerful sculptural quality, similar to the large-scale works of sculptor Richard Serra.

The Tyler House is located in Tubac, Arizona, about fifty miles south of Tucson and fifty miles north of the Mexican border. The clients fell in love with the site because of its dramatic views of terra-cotta-colored mountain ranges and open expanses that allow great views of summer lightning storms marching across the desert as well as the stars at night. The stargazing opportunities were especially important because the owners are astronomy buffs, as well as big fans of contemporary art and architecture.

The house is composed of two separate shedlike buildings slightly buried into a gently sloping hillside and separated by a courtyard. The larger block, totaling 2,500 square feet, contains a large, open living and dining room; a kitchen; a master suite; his and her offices; and a large covered porch (which looks and feels like an enormous outdoor living room) overlooking a swimming pool and the mountains beyond. The smaller, 1,500-square-foot structure houses a workshop, garage, and tiny guest quarters. The two blocks are angled to take advantage of specific views of the mountain range to the south. Visitors enter the compound along a gravel road, slightly above the level of the house, park the car, and descend along a wedge-shaped staircase into the courtyard between the two buildings, which frame the client's favorite views of Tumacacaori Peak.

The entire house is wrapped in large sheets of steel and topped with a roof of corrugated metal, both of which were left unsealed to turn a rich, rusty copper tone that echoes the colors of the desert landscape. The exterior is dotted with windows framing smaller vignettes of the expansive landscapes. Some windows pop out from the metal skin; other openings are punched out of the walls. The home's interiors are in a completely different character than its exterior, with polished concrete floors, smooth white plaster walls, clear and translucent glass panes, and maple paneling.

The Tyler home's low profile, angular roofs—and of course, its burnt metal color—help it blend almost seamlessly into the landscape of mountain peaks and mesquite trees, as well as into the architectural history of the Southwest desert.

Seen from a distance against a mountain backdrop, the Tyler House appears as a pair of rusty steel boxes nestled into the desert landscape. The volume at left houses a garage, workshop, and two guestrooms; at right is the main house, with a large shaded porch.

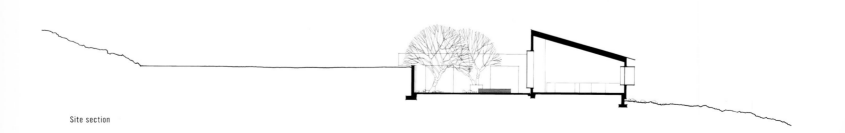

Site section

The house's rusted steel skin reflects changes in the desert light **(facing page, above left)**, while its steeply pitched roofs echo the profiles of the mountains surrounding Tubac, Arizona **(facing page, above right)**. Surrounding the house is a natural landscape of desert scrub and low mesquite brush **(above left)**. The approach to the house **(above right)** is along a dusty road above the house that winds down to a driveway leading to the separate garage. A section drawing **(facing page)** shows the change in level of the driveway above the main house, separated from the garage by a planted courtyard.

A floor-to-ceiling glass wall leads from the kitchen to the eastern end of the shaded terrace, with the granite-edged pool beyond **(above)**. A similar door at the opposite side of the kitchen leads to the western end of the terrace **(facing page, left)**. A hallway overlooks the interior courtyard **(facing page, center)**. A view down the open living and dining room ends in a view through a floor-to-ceiling glass wall **(facing page, right)**.

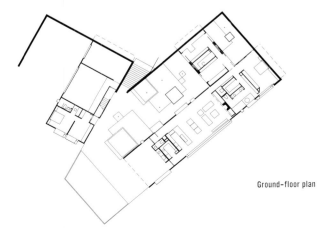

Ground-floor plan

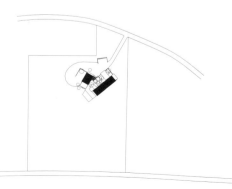

Site plan

The north-facing glass wall of the workshop, shaded by a deep overhang of the steel roof, peeks out from a cactus garden **(facing page, left)**. The angular roof overhang shelters an outdoor kitchen and dining terrace overlooking the pool **(facing page, right)**. A long rectangular opening cut out of the side wall, which frames desert views, creates the sensation of a large window opening into an outdoor room **(above)**. At left is the planted entry courtyard separating the main house from the garage and guestroom wing.

Alberto Kalach
GGG House
Chapultepec
Mexico City, Mexico
2000

The extensive use of concrete imparts a monastic, serene air to many works of modern architecture. Perhaps it is inevitable that such work evokes masterworks by Le Corbusier, Louis Kahn, Tadao Ando, and others who allowed concrete to liberate their design visions and vocabularies. These architects fully grasped and celebrated concrete's simplicity and malleability, strength and controllability, austerity and honesty.

Mexico City–based architect Alberto Kalach always wanted to build a concrete house. "You can make almost anything you want with a continuous concrete surface," he says, "and I like the idea of one material that can solve many different problems, such as the structure of big cantilevers." But, one must admit, concrete buildings can also be considered brutalist, oppressive, and cold. How many homeowners would give in to an architect's whim to see what formal inventions he could mold from such a rough, monotonous material? Concrete is not an obvious material choice in the domestic realm, where people naturally want surfaces that are warm to the eye and touch. Kalach was fortunate to find a client, an architecture buff, willing to let him pursue his longtime curiosity about constructing an entire house of concrete.

Concrete turned out to be an appropriate material for the GGG House, located in a wealthy neighborhood five miles outside of Mexico City's center. With sharp disparities between the economic classes in Mexico, it is not unusual for the city's more affluent houses and neighborhoods to be gated and guarded. The GGG House had to be secure and discrete. Kalach wanted it to feel like a haven, but not like a fortress. From the street, the house appears smaller than it is, with a narrow façade of telescoping concrete cubes. The façade is inscrutable and deceptively modest. Once entered, the house opens up completely, and luxuriously: A narrow entry bridge leads quickly to the sunny heart of the house, a double-height atrium court. It features a glazed-in picture garden, with a sculpture by Mexican artist Jorge Yazpik set in a reflecting pool. The stone is carved with voids alternating with mass. The sculpture is the house's centerpiece and its inspiration.

Like the sculpture, the house is kept to a limited material palette. By sticking to a single material, forms and spaces can be more deeply explored. While Kalach's method of poured-in-place concrete walls is fairly standard practice, his innovation is how he uses the planes to achieve complex spatial effects. In the sculpture and the house alike, surfaces flow continuously, as do spaces. Concrete planes float and interpenetrate, creating intimate and grand spaces that have views toward other parts of the house, the outdoors, and the sky above. The architect himself describes the house as a labyrinth.

From the central court, the house expands in all directions. On the ground floor, the kitchen, and the living and dining areas radiate around the central court and spill visually and physically to outside spaces—a terrace, another reflecting pool, a manicured lawn surrounded by lush flowering trees. A glass bridge floats over the light court and hints at the secret spaces that compose the house's upper level (mostly private quarters). Slits are incised on thick concrete walls, offering more sneak peaks, as do the windows, which are everywhere—mullionless, cornerless, buffed. Sliding doors, too, reconfigure rooms into pavilions or hallways. Walnut stairs turn a corner, disappearing. All of these elements complicate one's sense of the spaces, deepening the mystery of the house's arrangement.

As a foil for the rough concrete, Kalach chose extremely smooth and refined materials for other surfaces: fine walnut, abundant glass, and travertine marble. The result is a cool, contemplative house. Coolness is a desirable result in this house on the edge of Mexico City, distancing its dwellers from urban chaos just a few miles away, like the walled-in Spanish haciendas that guard against the hustle and bustle of the city outside its walls. Concrete's physical coolness, too, echoes the use of adobe in traditional Mexican building, as well as its modern interpretations (most notably by master Luis Barragan), tempering the hot weather and making one grateful for a house of light and shade, reflections and breezes.

Monolithic materially and without windows, the façade of the all-concrete GGG House is understated and inscrutable, defensive against unwanted attention as well as the southerly sun. With its telescoping volumes, the house also appears deceptively smaller than it is.

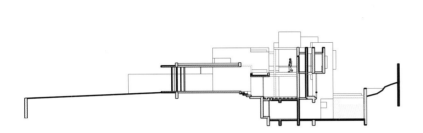

North-south section

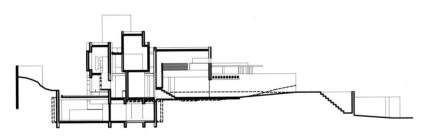

East-west section

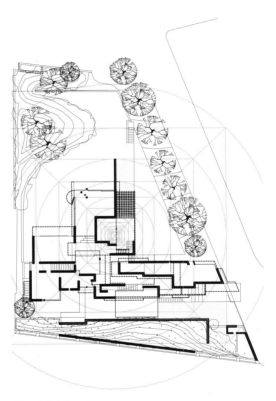

Site and first-floor plan

In contrast to its street façade, the house's rear opens up dramatically toward its garden and a projecting reflecting pool **(facing page)**. Kalach's play with planes creates variable openings, and inside the
house **(above)**, a veritable labyrinth. The entrance is at the right of the plan. The shared rooms, such as the kitchen and living rooms that open to outdoor terraces, are at the ground level, and the private rooms are at the
upper levels.

With its glazed walls slid completely open, the living room becomes an open-air pavilion. Kalach liked the idea of using concrete continuously throughout the house, for its ability to solve so many structural problems, such as large cantilevers.

The entire house is an exploration of transparency and opacity, with surprising views made possible by strategically placed glazing and deep slits incised on the thick concrete walls. These features deepen the mystery of the house and the arrangement of its spaces.

Three sculptures by Jorge Yazpik set in reflecting pools appear throughout the house. Yazpik's materially continuous forms served as an inspiration for the house; both are studies of mass and void.

View of the side of the house, leading toward the rear garden. Kalach contrasts the smooth, monotonous concrete with textured, rustic stone staircase.

From the narrow entrance foyer **(above left)**, one shoots toward the house's central open court, a glazed double-height shaft with a sculpture by Jorge Yazpik set in a reflecting pool **(above right)**. Overlooking the atrium court is a glazed bridge that links the second-level bedrooms. Yazpik's sculptures also appear outside the front entry, visible from the foyer **(facing page, above)** and the kitchen **(facing page, below)**.

Kalach chose refined materials, like travertine marble and walnut, to counter the roughness of the concrete. The house's many rooms and spaces form a labyrinth; carefully apportioned light filters into contemplative corners.

Tectonics Alberto Kalach, GGG House

Barton Myers Associates
Myers House
Montecito, California
1998

The idea of living in a metal house summons the austere attitude of the war and postwar era. Landmark applications of steel in houses such as Charles Eames's and Pierre Koenig's 1940s Case Study houses were born from a conservationist approach toward materials. They exploited off-the-shelf products to achieve economies of scale as well as structural and aesthetic progress. Architects comprise the bulk of the narrow market for such hard-edged solutions, however, as it remains difficult to convince most people to embrace materials that jar with the traditional sense of the domestic.

Barton Myers has created a compound of steel buildings, consisting of his own residence, studio, and a guesthouse, on a forty-site in the coastal Santa Barbara mountains. (This is not Myers's first steel home; in the 1970s he built himself a steel townhouse in Toronto.) This collection of buildings is primarily steel-and-glass boxes, straightforward in construction. The buildings step down the sloping site, interspersed with live oak trees; the roof for each doubles as a reflecting pool, making the buildings "disappear" from the views from the buildings above. Their most unconventional and innovative features are the buildings' façades. The principal walls are glazed, roll-up garage doors, certifying their kinship with open-air pavilions. Another layer of galvanized steel shutters are installed above every opening and can also be rolled down, sealing the buildings completely to provide security when the family is away, fire-protection in this fire-hazardous landscape, or thermal insulation.

To Myers, steel is an obvious material choice for any architect interested in structural clarity and lightness. The buildings are consequently airy, uninterrupted, and loftlike. (Each pavilion is similar in plan, with their front halves given over to vaulted common spaces and spilling onto terraces, and their back halves, contained in lower-ceiling volumes, allotted to more intimate or service-oriented rooms, such as bedrooms, kitchens, and bathrooms.) The orientation and siting of the buildings were determined to take advantage of ocean and mountain views. With such a picturesque site, it is obvious why Myers would want to create buildings with disappearing walls. Few would have suspected that heavy-duty industrial materials would be such great accomplices in enhancing the experience of a stunning environment.

The main house's façade is fronted with two layers of retractable garage doors—one glazed and the other galvanized steel. When the doors are rolled up, the building becomes an alfresco pavilion that extends the space of the patio and lap pool. Inside, the loftlike space contains the living room and kitchen/dining area.

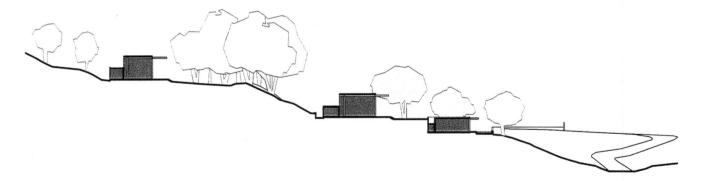

Site section

The house is actually a collection of three buildings that step down a sloping coastal mountain terrain. The architect's studio is at the top of the site **(site section plan, facing page)**, the main residence is at midlevel, and the guesthouse is at the bottom. Planes of water on the roof of the main house **(facing page, right)** conceal the structure from the building above it and also protects it from wildfires. The steel shutters that sheath the buildings also offer a degree of fire protection.

With the house's façade rolled up, opening toward an outdoor terrace with a fireplace, the lines between indoors and out are blurred. The living area is a vast loft, minimally separated from the kitchen by a low wall on one end **(facing page, left)**, and anchored by a fireplace on the other **(facing page, right)**. These large public rooms occupy the front part of the building **(ground-floor plan, facing page)**, while the bedrooms occupy a lower volume attached to the rear. The main house is at the middle of the sloping site, with the studio above it, and a guesthouse (with garage) below **(facing page, below left)**.

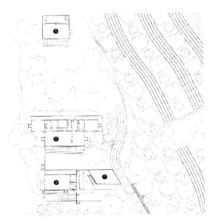

Site plan

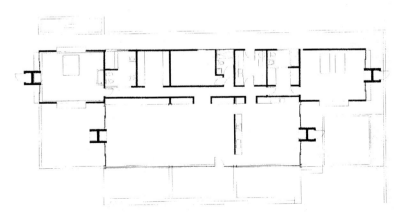

Ground-floor plan of the main residence

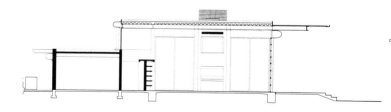

Section through main residence

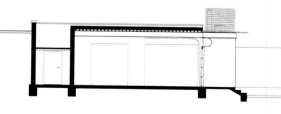

Section through guesthouse

Fire-resistant steel rolling shutters and windowed garage doors make an open-and-shut case for these flexible pavilion buildings **(facing page, left and right)**. The buildings are expedient constructions of steel and glass.

The guesthouse **(above and left)** shares the same features as the studio and main residence—rolling, disappearing façades that open to a private patio, equipped with an indoor-outdoor fireplace. All the buildings have a degree of privacy as a result of their careful siting.

Context

The bulk of houses produced in the United States has been stamped from the same neo-traditional templates for decades. Drive through almost any residential subdivision and witness a stylistic pastiche—an unnatural commingling of colonial mini-mansions, faux French chateaux, wood-shingled ranches, stuccoed haciendas, and other styles, transplanted from alien contexts and eras. In form, image, and function, these houses have little to do with where they are and who they serve.

This disregard for context—both physical and cultural—harkens to the flawed arguments for universality advanced by proponents of International Style modernism. Like the incongruous house types in the runaway subdivisions, high modernism ignored issues of locale—such as landscape, materials, climate, and lifestyle. In other words, it subverted much of what had been a natural part of traditional or vernacular building practices. But parallel to the rise of canonical modernism was the development of various other modernisms: From Eastern Europe to Latin America, architects over the last century have been producing distinctive modernist work that maintains some continuity with local traditions or values. This regional modernist approach is as concerned with technology, function, and economy as with the particularities of place. In 1947, critic Lewis Mumford praised regional modernism in a *New Yorker* article about Bay Area architecture (which he dubbed the "Bay Region style"), commending it as "far more truly a universal style than the so-called International Style...since it permits...adaptations and modifications."

Regionalism remains one of the most fruitful formulations of modernism, intensifying especially in recent decades, and acquiring new dimensions. After the 1960s, the idea became strongly aligned with environmentalism and social responsibility, for it implied a building approach that would impact the landscape and local culture as minimally as possible—and deepen the way we regard, experience, and value them. Though postmodernism in the 1970s, too, emphasized contextuality and historical continuity, these concerns were eventually manifested in little more than superficial visual motifs. Reducing local histories to ironic references and scenographic gimmicks, mainstream postmodernism ultimately obstructed, rather than contributed to, any genuine understanding of local traditions.

For the next decade, technological progress—of the sort that would impart technical innovations as well as economies of scale, social equity, and ecological values to architecture—stalled. As a reaction, by the early 1980s, a theory of "critical regionalism" began to emerge, articulated first by Liane Lefaivre and Alexander Tzonis and popularized by modernism's preeminent historian, Kenneth Frampton. He called for architecture based on technological innovation rather than imagery, making clear that such an approach integrated universal concerns such as function and cost, with local concerns for society, nature, and culture. Frampton was advocating not a revival of vernacular or historic building, but the development of architecture that was critically engaged with the present problem, in its present context, at its present time.

The houses in this chapter are inheritors of this tradition, illustrating the breadth of what a critical regionalist approach encompasses. Brian MacKay-Lyons's House #22 in a fishing village in Nova Scotia appears at first to be anything but sensitive to context, for it sticks out like a square sore thumb among its neighboring quaint pitch-roofed cottages. But this hemlock- and metal-sided house has gleaned from vernacular building practices: Its durable, noncorrosive metal cladding and simple boxy forms mediate the harsh, damp climate. For many of the houses MacKay-Lyons has built in his native Nova Scotia, he is careful about how to use wood, applying lessons from boat-building (with boards nailed on one side only, anticipating how wood shrinks and expands). His deep understanding of local material culture—of why and how materials are assembled—contributes to his buildings' ability to perform and age well. They are also economical: "If you tap into the vernacular method of doing things, which is very rich here, you can get a lot of stuff built cheap," he observes.

Maintaining continuities with local material culture is economical as well as ecological, for it saves on the costs and pollution associated with transporting resources from afar. Think of Finnish Alvar Aalto's reliance on wood and Colombian Rogelio Salmona's predilection for brick. These are acts of resourcefulness—and of poetry, for local materials resonate with the existing built and natural landscape. Architects David Lake and Ted Flato of Lake/Flato consciously decided to use local granite for the Bartlit House in Castle Pines, Colorado, for exterior and interior walls and floors. The effect is that the house appears a natural part of its rocky mountain outcropping, not an imposition on it.

The Bartlit House blends into the land, as does Alberto Kalach and Daniel Alvarez's Casa Negro outside Mexico City. In both cases, the topography and unique characteristics of the land determine the houses' form, massing, and circulation. The Bartlit House is backed into a natural draw in the mountainside, and thus feels sheltered by the site, borrowing a sense of solidity from the boulders which actually penetrate into the house. The rooms extend to outdoor terraces, enhancing a sense of seamlessness between the house and its surroundings. Meanwhile, Casa Negro insinuates itself into its heavily forested site, with a series of broken-up volumes that zig-zag down the hillside. In other words, the site modulates the form of the house, and gives logic to its organic arrangement. The five independent wings are devoted to unique uses, such as common rooms, kitchen, bedrooms, and studio, with the roofs of lower volumes serving as pathways and terraces. The house interweaves exterior and interior spaces and reminds the inhabitants at every turn that they are living in an Eden.

Both these architecture firms did not shy away from complexity, preferring to break down the houses, increasing the number of volumes and designing in odd configurations, rather than plant single, large monolithic objects on their pristine sites.

Similarly, Mack Scogin Merrill Elam Architects' Nomentana House in Lovell, Maine, and Miller/Hull Partnership's Michaels-Sisson House on Mercer Island, Washington, are sited so as to minimize disruption to their surroundings. But both these houses make no attempt to blend in with the landscape. In fact, they might strike many as jarring "machines in the gardens." Still, they do have a conservationist ethic: The vertical boxiness of the Michaels-Sisson House was driven by a desire to preserve as many trees as possible. According to Robert Hull, they approached the building site by asking, "What's the least we can do?" Likewise, the spindly, angular, projecting Nomentana House was carefully woven through the trees, hovering above the wooded sloping site. Though the houses are dramatic objects in themselves, the architects in both instances were keen to maximize their buildings' relationship to the landscape. Both houses were also driven by an impulse to exploit patterns of wind and light, as well as views.

The idea of framing views is extended in Wendell Burnette's Schall House in Phoenix. Behind the curving street façade of this house is a compound of rooms, terraces, courtyards, and balconies that are oriented around the surrounding desert vistas. Strategic windows excise perfect pictures of the horizon, while cutting off views of the dense, unbecoming suburb immediately outside the house's walls. The design is an accumulation of selective, contextual editing, a fortress against "visual pollution," explains the architect. The house heightens the residents' respect and awareness of the beauty of its location.

A contextual approach is inherently sustainable. Before air-conditioning, artificial lighting, and other modern building technology, builders had to pay attention to siting, orientation, materials, the consumption of energy, and the production of waste—otherwise their work would suffer the worst effects of climate swings, sun exposure, and deterioration. These practices emerged from our natural inclination to depend on the resources at hand, and desire to create works of lasting value. Today, these practices continue out of necessity in places of poverty—and out of intelligence in places of wealth. In a world of depleting natural resources, increasing pollution, and homogenizing cultural forces, architecture can be a force in conserving resources, society, and identity. The houses in this chapter extend the wisdom of pre-modern building, while continuing the ongoing modernist project of exploring appropriate technological innovations.

Mack Scogin Merrill Elam Architects
Nomentana House
Lovell, Maine
1998

Visitors entering the Nomentana House in rural Maine are faced with a hard-core modernist collage of white boxes and sleek expanses of glass. But as they step from the entry walkway, across an arched footbridge and beneath a zinc canopy, and through the front door, the home starts to reveal a different, unexpected character. The rocky ground drops away quickly and the house changes from a rigid, boxy structure into a sharp, angular one lifted into the trees on spindly steel and wood columns.

Atlanta architects Mack Scogin, Merrill Elam, and Lloyd Bray designed the house for an artist/interior designer who relocated from Los Angeles. The architects saw the scenic woodland site as delicate and wanted to disrupt the natural setting as little as possible. So they drew a line in the sand, so to speak, to divide the site into two distinct areas. The line, a low concrete curb along the driveway, distinguishes between the parts of the house that sit directly on relatively flat ground—the garage and the owner's painting studio—and the rest of the house, which hovers above the wooded, rocky slope on slender columns. By raising the house above the ground, the designers were able to thrust it up into the trees in order to maximize the views of its wooded surroundings. This strategy helped them disrupt the site minimally, while allowing its owner to feel close to nature.

Just inside the entry foyer is a two-story, open-air shaft wrapped by sheer glass walls and steel-plated stairs and bookshelves. Behind this light shaft is a long corridor that links the two wings of the pinwheel-plan house. One wing contains the master bedroom and bath with a small, screened sleeping porch; the other houses a dining room, separate living room, and kitchen. There is a small porch adjoining the kitchen and a larger one, located beneath the angular, prow-shaped end of the house, located off the living room. The pointy terrace is turned to face an unspoiled view of a lake. Upstairs are a guest bedroom with an adjoining flagstone-paved terrace on one side of the house and a private study on the other, which is revealed on the exterior as a little freestanding box perched on metal stilts.

Though the floor plans are full of quirky bumps and boxes and a boldly angled terrace, the quirks are all for good reason. They take advantage of a particular view out into the woods, and allow glimpses from one part of the house back into another and then outside again, to a different part of the site. Even the mysterious glass tower ringed with books and stairs has a relation to the site: it allows light and creates the illusion of rain or snow falling right into the heart of the house.

The materials are fairly tough and industrial—perforated and bent steel plates, zinc, glass, and concrete-fiberboard—but they are neutral enough to let the woods and the changing patterns of light by day or season influence the nature of the house.

The thin steel columns that lift the Nomentana House above a forested hillside in Maine recall the site's slender trees. A large, angular terrace projects beyond the house and into the trees, facing a lake.

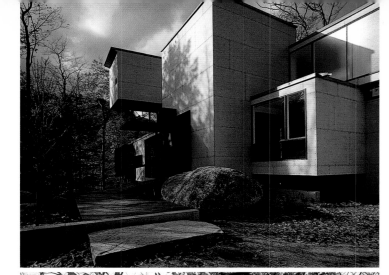

Seen from the driveway, the house gives the impression of being a rigid assembly of white boxes, reminiscent of early European modernist architecture **(left)**. As one moves around the house, how-ever, the boxy composition loosens up, as the house becomes angular and freeform **(images at right)**. The owner's private study is a semi-attached box perched on stilts, seen from the entry path, which leads to an arched concrete foot-bridge **(above right)**. On the west side, a large, flared chimney projects from the bed-room wing **(center right)**. Behind the solid, cement-board wall adjoining the sharply angled terrace is the living room **(below right)**.

Context Mack Scogin Merrill Elam Architects, Nomentana House

North-south section looking east through master bedroom and entry/library

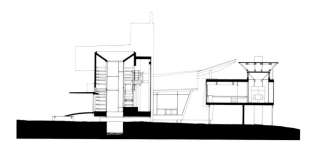

North-south section looking west through entry/library and master bedroom

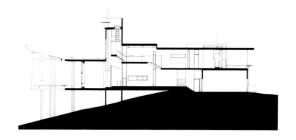

East-west section looking north through living room/chimney tower and guest bedroom

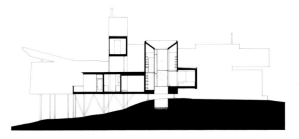

East-west section looking north through entry/library and drawing studio

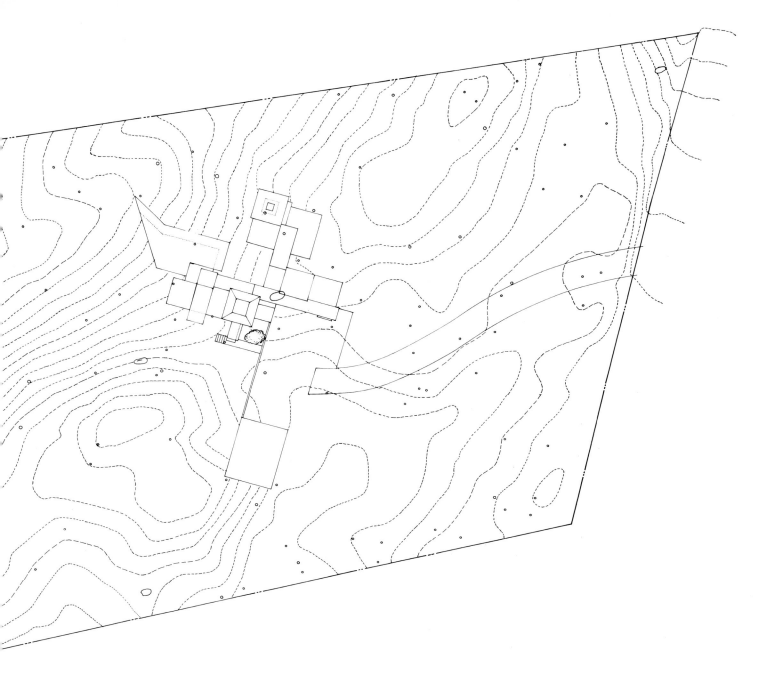

Site plan

The site plan **(above)** shows the entry to the house is along a driveway on the gently sloping part of the property **(at right)**. The house, which is arranged around an internal courtyard defined on three sides, sits where the landscape starts to suddenly slope downhill. Sections through the house **(facing page)** show how it sits on piers, or pilotis, as the landscape slopes away from the building. The tall internal light shaft, visible as it extends above the rest of the house, is wrapped by a staircase and bookshelves.

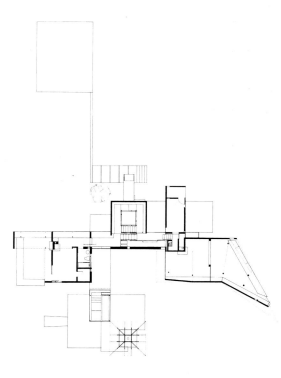

Second-floor plan

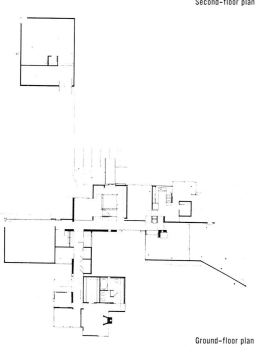

Ground-floor plan

The pointy terrace off the living room opens onto prime views of a nearby lake. The terrace's walls are made of cement board panels with exposed bolts; the floor is made of irregularly patterned flagstone.

The living room **(left)** features a large fireplace at its center and cement fiber-board walls. Windows along the east façade overlook an interior courtyard created by the house's winding floor plan. The furnishings are as spare and dramatic as one would expect for such an aggressive house. The master bed-room **(above right)** features a seat along windows that wrap a cor-ner to take advantage of the forest views and opens onto a small terrace. The kitchen offers a glimpse of the site through an angled skylight and glass wall **(below right)**.

At the heart of the house is a tough industrial stair flanking two stories of bookshelves **(above left and right)**. The staircase wraps around a narrow, interior courtyard modeled after the impluvium of ancient Roman homes that brings light and rain into the center of the house **(below left)**. Along one side of the stair is a long corridor linking the front and back parts of the house.

Wendell Burnette Architects
Schall House
Phoenix, Arizona
1999

The nonstop growth of Phoenix, Arizona, is one of the worst examples of suburban sprawl in the United States. The city is spreading out in all directions and gobbling up acres of native desert at an alarming rate, replacing the delicate natural landscape with a sea of faux-Spanish houses with red-tile roofs. Despite this encroaching invasion of what locals bitterly call "Taco Bells," the city's natural features still remain: dramatic mountain ranges and colorful vegetation. Capturing views of all this natural beauty and making homes that truly take advantage of everything the climate offers is still a concern for local architects.

One such architect, Wendell Burnette, designed a hilltop house for a retired engineer and his wife that maximizes views of mountains and city while minimizing the influence of the surrounding suburban sprawl. Burnette looked to the inwardly focused urban courtyard houses of North Africa—an appropriate source of inspiration, given Arizona's similarly arid climate—as an effective strategy for capturing the best of all possible worlds.

The 2,200-square-foot house is located on a cul-de-sac at the northernmost end of Central Avenue, Phoenix's north-south spine, cradled between neighboring Spanish-style houses and the ridges of a narrow canyon. From its hillside perch, the site commands views of the vast city below, as well as the peaks of the Sierra Estrella Mountains beyond. Burnette designed the house as an almost impenetrable curving hulk of concrete block sheltering a cool, quiet interior courtyard. He inserted windows exactly where he wanted to capture worthwhile views: Long bands of glass, such as the windows in the living room and dining room, frame broad but narrow panoramas of the city and faraway mountains, while larger, square windows are oriented toward views of the immediate landscape.

Visitors arriving by car—the way most people in the car-crazed Sun Belt would—enter into a sheltered gravel driveway at the short end of the whale-shaped house. Adjoining the driveway is a single-auto carport and an enclosed two-car garage, as well as a pair of guestrooms overlooking the craggy hillside behind the house. The rest of the ground floor is filled with a terrace, a fragrant desert garden, and a long, rectangular pool that form a tranquil oasis at the heart of the home. The careful placement of masonry walls around this inner courtyard effectively edits out the undesirable surroundings without eliminating the desirable views; when you are in this outdoor space, you completely forget that you are in the middle of endless suburban sprawl. Openings in the wall let light and cross-breezes fill the courtyard.

The main living quarters are located a full story up, and are accessible either by a sleek, industrial elevator that opens onto the courtyard (one of the owners suffers from hip problems) or by a mysterious winding staircase that wraps along the curving west façade of the house. The elevator deposits visitors in the middle of the dining room; the stairs end at a small terrace that opens onto the dining area. The rest of the airy upper-level living space includes a living room at the west end, with views of the city and of the courtyard and garden below, and a large master suite at the east end. The interior finishes are simple—wooden floors made of salvaged maple planks and white walls—but Burnette's conscious placement of windows helps fill the spaces with bright but subtle light.

The Schall House's billowing, whalelike profile creates a mysterious entry elevation. The entrance to a semi-enclosed carport and garage is at the far, short end of the home. An apparently random pattern of small square windows and thin slits in the concrete block skin frame specific views from the inside and create moody washes of desert light inside.

Behind the curving entry façade is what appears to be an entirely different house made of rectangular planes of whitewashed concrete nestled up against a desert hillside. The house is organized around a long pool and a small garden, an oasis from the suburban sprawl of Phoenix. The main living spaces are located on the second floor.

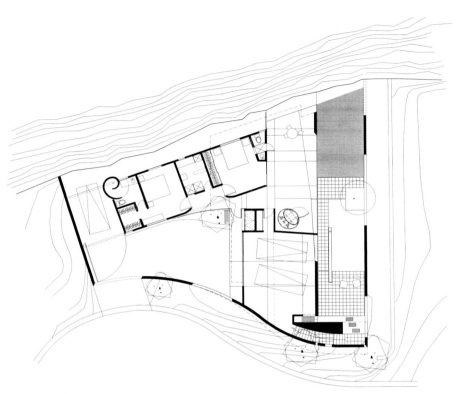

Ground-floor plan

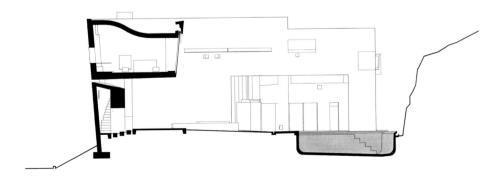

Section through living space and pool courtyard

A large, east-facing window in the living room overlooks the secluded courtyard **(facing page)**, which is screened off from the neighbors by a wall. A circular elevator **(above left)** provides easy access to the second-floor living spaces. Beneath the overhanging volume containing the living room is a shaded outdoor dining area facing the parched desert hillside **(above right)**.

A winding staircase located behind the curving concrete-block entry façade creates a mysterious path up to the second-floor living spaces. Carefully placed openings in the wall—some long and thin, others square—let in controlled sunlight and offer edited views of the surroundings.

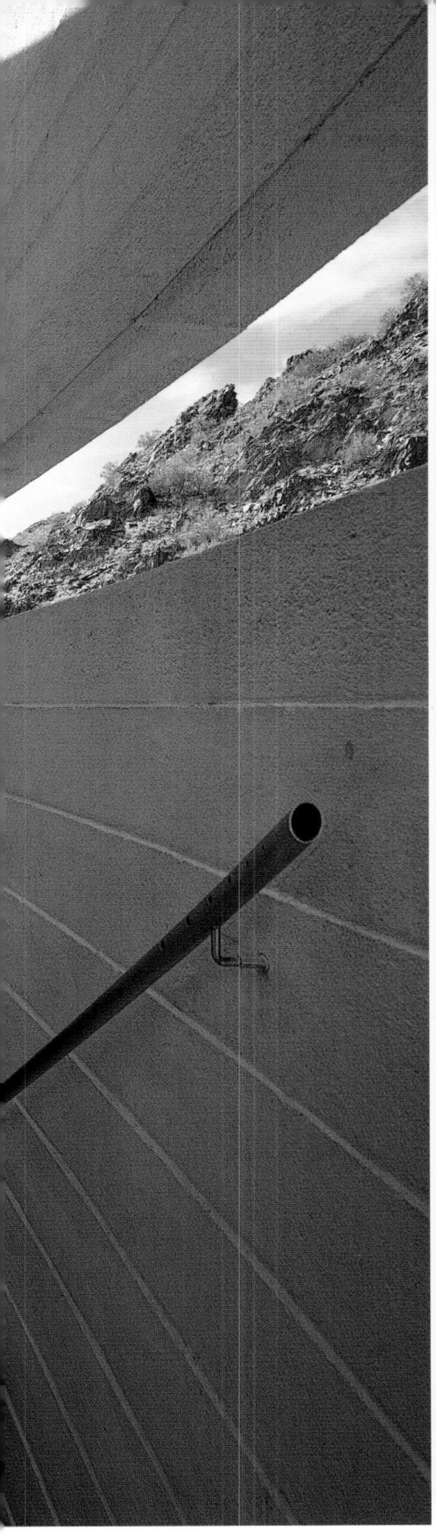
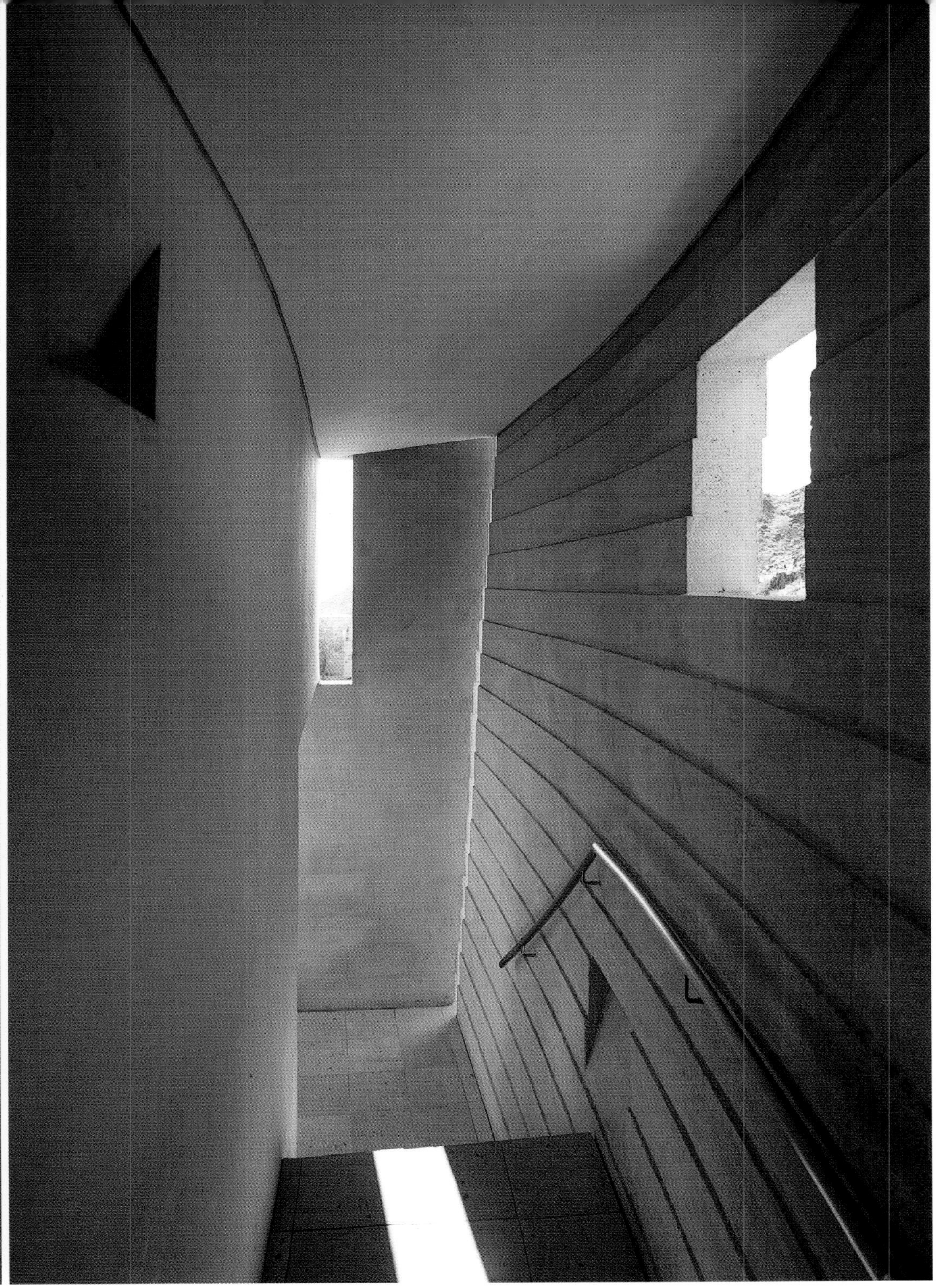

Purposefully placed window openings in the living room **(facing page, above and below)**, dining room **(above left)**, and master bedroom **(above right)** control the harsh desert sun that would ordinarily make these south-facing rooms uncomfortable in summer and offer carefully framed views of the natural and manmade landscape. The home's modern furnishings are deliberately simple, to let the play of light and views become the primary focus. An east-facing sliding glass door in the master bedroom **(above right)** leads to a small terrace, which is shaded in the mornings by the adjoining hillside.

se glows mysteriously as light escapes from the random pattern of windows and openings in the otherwise solid concrete–block skin. The blocky volume of the living spaces is visible just above the curve the distance is the nighttime skyline of Phoenix.

Alberto Kalach and Daniel Alvarez
Casa Negro
Contadero
Mexico City, Mexico
1999

Designed by architects Alberto Kalach and Daniel Alvarez, Casa Negro in the leafy suburbs of Mexico City is the ultimate hillside home. Many designers struggle with the problems of building a house on a sloping site; often their solution is to perch the building over the hill or bury it into the earth. (Frank Lloyd Wright did both better than anyone in the design of his masterful Fallingwater in Bear Run, Pennsylvania.) Kalach and Alvarez took a strikingly different approach: They broke the 7,500-square-foot home into five separate volumes and set the pieces tumbling down a steep, thickly forested hillside. One wanders down the hill along a series of interior and exterior stairs and platforms, often using the roof of the structure beneath as a pathway.

Visitors enter the house near the top of the hill, into a volume containing a long foyer and separate living and dining rooms; an adjoining box uphill houses the kitchen and servants' quarters. At the end of the long hallway, one descends along a staircase into another, separate volume containing an informal living room and a suite of bedrooms—a master suite and two children's rooms. The roof of this bedroom block doubles as a terrace off the living and dining rooms above. To move down the hillside from the bedrooms, one must venture outdoors: An external staircase leads to a private, two-story study and exercise area, and beyond that is another staircase leading to the pool, the finale of the winding, indoor-outdoor promenade.

This interweaving of interior and exterior connections makes its inhabitants acutely aware of how precipitous the site is—it is impossible to move down the hillside from one wing of the house to another without seeing the steep slope. Not only can you see the naturally dense vegetation that the architects were careful to maintain through large expanses of floor-to-ceiling glass; you actually get to—literally—walk among the treetops. The interior staircase connecting the living areas and the bedrooms makes sense functionally; the exterior stairs leading to the study and pool are not completely impractical, given Mexico City's year-round mild climate.

Although the zig-zagging downhill sequence through the house's various pieces is fixed, the circulation through each volume is fluid. The living and dining rooms, for example, are really part of the same loftlike volume, divided only by concrete walls that stop short of the ceiling of exposed wooden beams. The corridor linking the three bedrooms is wrapped in glass, giving the feeling of walking along an open-air trellis. In fact, the house is filled with huge glass walls extending the entire height of the structure and often wrapping corners, creating the sensation that the home has no exterior walls.

The home's materials are highly polished and well crafted, but earthy enough to tie the house to its forested surroundings. There are concrete walls, walls made of ochre-colored soil excavated from the site, and limestone walls; heavy wooden doors; and warm wood floors and ceilings that contrast more high-tech elements like the glazed façades and steel stair railings.

Architect Alberto Kalach created a hillside promenade from the different wings of the 7,500-square-foot home he designed for a family outside Mexico City. A staircase from the living and dining wing **(at top in photo)** leads to a terrace atop the roof of a separate bedroom wing, just downhill. All around the hillside home are thick woods of native tepozan trees.

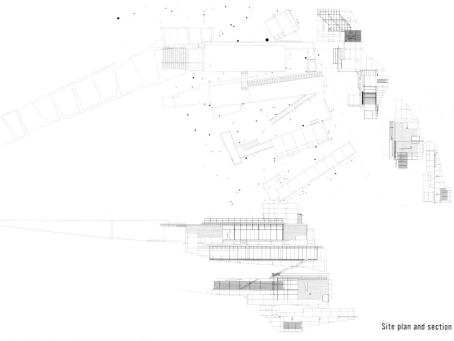

The site plan **(left)** and aerial view **(below left)** reveals the complicated sequence of pieces stepping down the hillside. From top to bottom: kitchen, living wing, bedroom wing, studio, and lap pool. The living and dining rooms are held in a volume clad in smooth sheets of glass and limestone **(right)**. The kitchen and servants' rooms are held in a tall box at the top of the hill **(far right)**.

Site plan and section

The entrance to the house is a pivoting, heavy wood door opening onto a secluded court **(top left)**. A hallway leading to the bedrooms feels like a greenhouse with expansive glass walls and ceiling that heighten the connections to the outside **(bottom left)**. These rooms are filled with light through horizontal strips of glass overlooking the wooded hillside. The exposed construction of wood and steel beams resting atop concrete walls complements the richly stained wood floor and sleek, minimal furnishings **(right)**.

The wooden path leading to the lap pool, the bottommost element of the home, passes through the two-story studio **(facing page)**. The studio's tall ceilings and huge expanses of glass overlooking the wooded hillside create the sensation that it is an open-air structure **(left)**. A series of combined plans, sections, and elevations of the different wings of the home **(right)** reveals the complex and constantly changing character of the house.

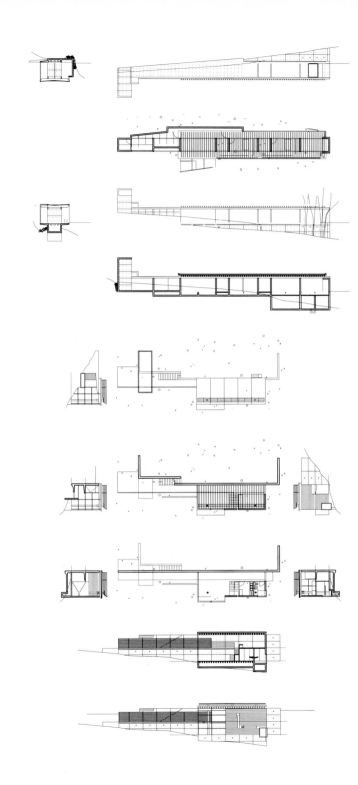

The long, winding path through the house ends in a wooden walkway that leads to the blue-tiled lap pool cantilevered beyond the hill **(right)**. A shallow reflecting pool atop the bedroom wing further uphill **(facing page)** reflects the trees and nighttime lights of the living and dining rooms.

Brian MacKay–Lyons
Architecture Urban Design
House #22
Oxner's Head
Nova Scotia, Canada
1999

Nova Scotia is a maritime idyll, featuring sparsely populated villages with quaint shingled fishing shacks and farmhouses. Its most prolific architect, Brian MacKay-Lyons, knows the landscape well, having practiced in Halifax for the last twenty years. In the manner of the best modernist-regionalists, his work is undeniably attuned to local traditions but as inquisitive of technique, material, and form as any rigorous modern project.

Designed for a couple, House #22 rises up on the crown of a small hill overlooking Canada's Atlantic shore. Though it appears bold and exposed, it is rooted in the land in demeanor and detail. The house is actually a pair of houses, a larger main house and a smaller detached guesthouse, on respective drumlins (glacial hills). They are sited about 450 feet apart on a north-south axis, paralleling the agrarian grid of the region's farmland. The natural wetland formed between the drumlins becomes the central garden between the two buildings. Though axial, the houses play against the natural undulating topography.

The straightforward construction, organization, and material of the two buildings acknowledge their roots in the utilitarian vernacular. Meanwhile, their cubic forms and quirky details are comparatively abstract in the context of pitch-roofed cottages. The faded gray, rough-hewn hemlock siding clads the top floors, a tough wrapper against the rain and a nod to the utilitarian wooden sheds and boat-building traditions in the area. Concrete floors and walls, and upper levels sheathed in corrugated metal are heavier-duty gestures that acknowledge that houses in Nova Scotia must constantly battle the harsh weather.

With nearly identical façades, both houses have concrete walls that project outward, pointing toward each other. Parallel to these are oversized roof scuppers that drain onto the stainless steel benches cantilevered from the walls. The attenuated walls and scuppers emphasize the houses' continuation of each other, and the sense of progression between the two.

Approaching the houses, one reaches the main house first, and enters to find a double-height living room and a clear view of the guesthouse beyond. Wood reappears inside: These structures are unfinished, finger-jointed, folk-tech timber frame. Trusses are left exposed, contributing to the room's feeling of openness. The circulation spine of the main house points to that of the guesthouse, which has basically the same floorplan. Symmetry aside, the experience of each house differs in the views: The main house looks back toward the village, and the other, to the ocean. Together, the houses narrate the landscape—360-degree views of the natural and manmade history that informs MacKay-Lyons's work.

This simple, modernist cottage is set upon a hill overlooking a small fishing village at the banks of the Atlantic Ocean. The architect employed simple forms, building techniques, and materials, as a response to local conditions and traditions. Noncorrosive corrugated metal siding clads the first floor, well suited to Nova Scotia's harsh climate. Wooden siding wraps the second floor, a reference to the local vernacular of wood-shingled houses.

The house is actually two buildings, a larger main residence (in the distance) and a smaller guesthouse **(above)**. Both are nearly identical in appearance, plan, and construction. On the main house **(facing page)**, an oversized roof scupper drains onto a stainless-steel bench that cantilevers from the concrete-block wall. The guesthouse has the same projecting features, which point directly at each other.

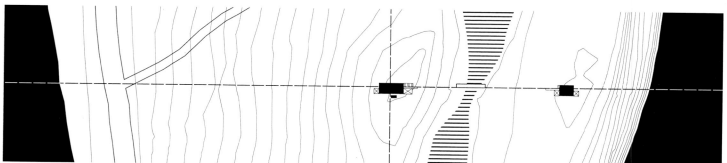

Site plan

Both houses have similar floor plans (facing page, below): The circulation spine for both is on one axis, with the living rooms opening to one side, and the narrow kitchen (above left) on the other. Materials, used inside and out, are kept simple. Leaving trusses exposed the second-floor master bedroom (facing page) makes the room more spacious. The two buildings are sited 450 feet apart with a natural wetland "garden" between them (site plan, above).

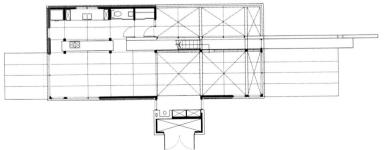

Ground-floor plan for main residence

Ground-floor plan for guesthouse

Context Brian MacKay-Lyons Architecture Urban Design, House #22

Inside the main house, the exposed, unfinished, diagonal hemlock trusses open up the living room **(facing page and above)**, clearing views to the guesthouse beyond and the spectacular surroundings. The approach is economical as well as appropriate to its context.

Miller/Hull Partnership
Michaels–Sisson House
Mercer Island, Washington
1998

To consider a boxy metal-sheathed house in the middle of a lush forest a contextual work of architecture might seem a conceptual stretch. But the Michaels-Sisson House, located on a tight woodsy site on Mercer Island, a suburb of Seattle, is critically engaged with both the immediate landscape and the tradition of Pacific Northwest architecture.

The house, designed by Seattle-based Miller/Hull Partnership, nestles into the site's slope and rises vertically, for the owners were determined to preserve as many of the old-growth evergreens as possible. Only three trees were removed to build this 1,960-square-foot house, preserving more trees than a plan by previous owners for a more horizontal house on the same site. Miller/Hull backed the house into the hill, setting its foundation deep against it. The house's lower level, containing the garage and children's rooms, is made of concrete blocks and actually doubles as a retaining wall.

To counter the potential for the lower-level rooms to be dark, glass squares and operable windows are punched through the concrete block façade. Their arrangement enlivens the lower portion of the house, which could otherwise resemble an oversized foundation wall. The windows also carve carefully framed views from within the house; their proportions are as calculated as the long vertical window that spans the upper two floors. As within a treehouse, tree branches graze the building's walls and windows. From inside, the view toward the outside is all green.

The upper half of the house is wrapped in unfinished corrugated steel, which will weather to a dull, natural shade. The more public rooms—kitchen, living, and dining rooms—are on the third floor, which opens to the hillside at the back with a serenely private wooden deck. The top floor is the master bedroom and a study. The rear façade features an enormous steel moment frame, which provides full-height windows for the third-floor living area and the top-floor master bedroom suite. The steel frame is designed to carry the seismic load for the house when an earthquake hits.

The rooms of the house are compact and simply finished, consistent with the exterior treatment. Exposed laminated wooden beams support the ceiling and floors are plain fiberboard—as uncomplicated and cozy as a treehouse. To alleviate the compactness of the interior, the third-floor living room looks out to the deck through a 9-by-10-foot window that is rigged with garage-door hardware and tension springs to enable it to slide straight upward. The house is completely open to the forest, in more ways than one.

This house was built on a tight site and a tight budget, on woodsy Mercer Island, Washington. Intent on disrupting the natural environment as minimally as possible (only three of the many old-growth evergreens were removed), the architects designed a compact, vertical house that is backed into the hillside. The concrete block enclosure of the lower two levels functions as a retaining wall.

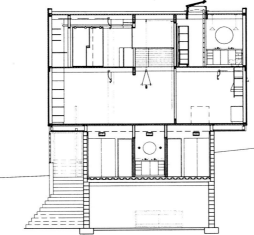

North-south section

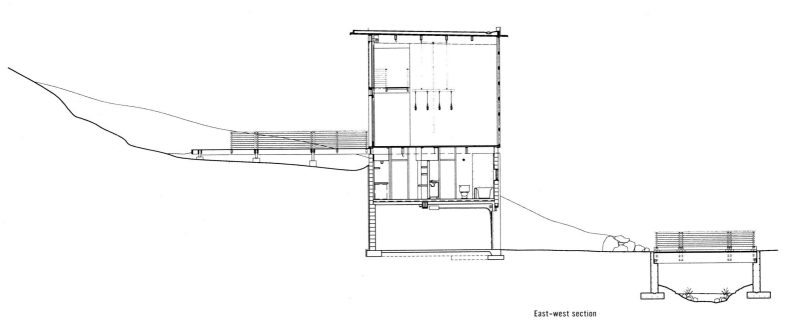

East-west section

Following the slope of the site, the house's ground level is a garage, leading to a bridge that spans a creek. Above the garage are the children's bedrooms, with glass blocks and operable windows enlivening the concrete-block walls **(facing page)**. The living room and kitchen occupies the third floor, and the master bedroom suite is stacked above it. The top two levels of the house are wrapped in unfinished corrugated metal, which will weather to a dull, natural shade.

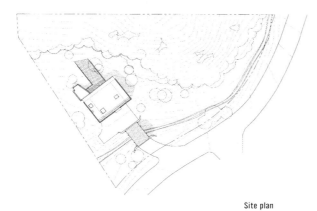

Site plan

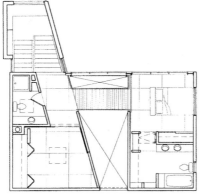

Fourth-floor plan

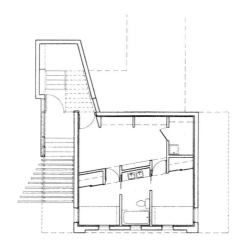

Second-floor plan

The steel moment frame of the rear façade allows full-height windows for the third-floor living spaces and the top-floor master bedroom suite **(facing page)**. It also acts as a seismic anchor for the house. The living room opens to a deck that leads toward the wooded slope at the house's rear. On the fourth floor **(left, center plan)**, the master bedroom overlooks the rear deck. The second floor **(below)** contains two small bedrooms and a larger playroom.

Context Miller/Hull Partnership, Michaels-Sisson House

The tall volume clad in corrugated metal contains the stairwell and lends privacy to the rear deck **(above left)**. The rooms inside are compact and simply finished, in keeping with the industrial materials used on the exterior. In the living room **(below left and facing page)**, the redtrimmed, three-panel glass door slides up vertically, with the help of garage door hardware and tension springs, opening the living room completely to the deck.

Using space judiciously, the architects tucked a small office space into the stair landing between the third and fourth floors **(right)**. A bridge leads to the master bedroom **(facing page)**. Wood ceilings and walls give the house a warm feel, like that of a treehouse.

Context Miller/Hull Partnership, Michaels-Sisson House

Lake/Flato Architects
Bartlit House
Castle Pines, Colorado
2000

The Bartlit House by San Antonio–based Lake/Flato Architects was not so much built on its rocky three-acre mountain site as it was inserted into it. For the architects, a natural draw (a dry creek bed) seemed the logical place to begin: They aligned the house's entryway with the old draw and straddled the house across it, using it as a natural divide for the house's two primary wings. The two wings are a series of rooms that spread out in various manners: burrowing into the hillside to the house's rear (east), opening to terraces and views to the front (west), and carving out intimate spaces in between.

So integrated is the house in the landscape that much of its organization was worked out on site. No section drawings were created. The house's complex composition of small, disparate, low volumes was generated by Lake/Flato's desire to take maximum advantage of the existing landscape, and its natural views and quirks. The house appears and disappears—its camouflage intensified by its rustic granite walls (the architects were keen on using Colorado granite) and, for some sections of the building, sod roofs. So complete is this house's merge with its landscape, that much of its 10,000 square feet is virtually invisible from the street above.

Partners David Lake and Ted Flato, whose 1990 Carraro House in Kyle, Texas, was widely publicized as an exemplar of regional modern architecture, are known to approach projects by starting with the landscape. At the same time, they are hardly slaves of it, applying spatial and technical ideas that ultimately work to the benefit of landscape and building alike. The Bartlit House capitalizes on views and follows the topography of the land but also creates practical, livable, and pleasurable spaces, such as the privacy-driven, semi-detached master bedroom suite, or the space-buffing, picture-window courtyard garden, or the indoor-outdoor terraces that extend the house to its scenic property.

To accentuate the seamlessness between the architecture and its surroundings, granite from nearby quarries (including some from the site itself) is used for walls and flooring, bleeding from indoors to out. Several boulders have also been left around the entryway and in the master bedroom for poetic effect, reminiscent of Frank Lloyd Wright's boulder at the river level of Fallingwater. Along the facing sides of the long gallery connecting the two wings are two massive rolling doors. When opened, the entire midsection of the house becomes an alfresco pavilion, with a small pool to one side and a large terrace to the other, taking in distant views of the Rocky Mountains.

To counter the heat gain and the light glare that would have resulted during the summertime from such expansive western views, the house has broad six-foot overhangs. Meanwhile, in the winter, the thermal mass of the interior granite walls are the source of passive solar heating; all pavilion rooms have southern solar exposure coupled with thick walls; and the guest wing's earthen roofs help also with passive climate control. The Bartlit House is an example in which the architecture works for the site, as much as the site works for the architecture.

The architects insinuated the house into its rocky mountain site rather than planting it on top of it, for they were reluctant to disturb the natural beauty of the surrounding landscape. Rustic walls made of local granite give the house the appearance of growing out of the land, while broken-up volumes contribute to its low-key appearance. Parts of the house (facing the street) are covered with sod roofs, which further camouflage the house from view.

The house is entered from the east (top of the plan on facing page) and opens entirely on its western side (bottom of the plan), toward views of the Rocky Mountain. The house is composed of two wings separated by a long gallery. On the northern wing (left of the plan) is the main living room, kitchen, and dining area, which is separated from the master bedroom suite by a garden courtyard. The southern wing (right of the plan) contains the guest bedrooms. The north wing's living room is an expansive glass pavilion, with an unpainted steel structure and gapped wood ceilings (above). The house is an assemblage of volumes linked by pathways and courtyards (facing page).

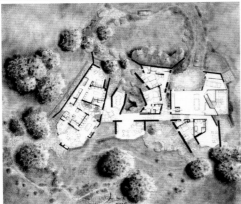

Site plan

The house's form, massing, and siting are strongly oriented around views. It opens up at multiple points, excising perfect vistas of the Rocky Mountains **(facing page)**. The vaulted ceiling of the glazed living room broadens views toward the sky and treetops **(above)**. The structure is left exposed, in order to free the interior of visual clutter. The lightness of the steel and glass contrasts with the heaviness of the stone used throughout.

The architects specified Colorado granite to maintain some connection to the local terrain. The weighty granite walls, which continue from the exterior to the interior, emphasize the idea that the house is firmly rooted to its context. Warmly tinted sandstone flooring accentuates the house's earthy, natural feel **(above)**. Almost every room in the house opens to an outside space **(facing page, left)**. A long hallway connects the two wings of the house **(facing page, right)**, which spread along the length of a mountain ridge, to maximize its western exposure.

The southern end of the house contains a guest bedroom, which opens to its own private terrace **(above)**. The harsh summer sun is tempered by six-foot overhangs along the west-facing terraces **(facing page)**. The house exploits many passive solar techniques like shading, low-emissivity glass, and earthen roofs (in the guest-wing), which eliminates the need for cooling. Meanwhile, the granite walls provide thermal mass.

Revolutions

What can we learn from observing how we live? Everything, according to anthropologists. The house gives form to our daily rituals—how we spend our time at home, resting, playing, working, and how we interact with our family, friends, and neighbors. Which room is the largest in the house? Which is the most trafficked, or the least? How do the rooms relate to each other? Are the parents' quarters as close to the children's rooms as possible, or as far away? How much privacy do we need, from fellow family members and from the world outside? All these answers vary—they are as unique as we are.

Houses are as much about shelter as they are about personal expression: Like our clothes, they disclose our tastes, lifestyles, habits, and values. Given how much these differ, it is unsettling how similar most houses are. The mass production of houses is governed by economies and averages, not by particularities and personalities. What is especially surprising, however, is how little houses have changed over time, considering the significant revolutions lifestyles have undergone, even just in the last thirty years. The average household has shifted from the traditional nuclear family to an array of configurations of human relations, reflecting the evolution of the definition of "family" itself: Unmarried couples, same-sex couples, single or divorced parents, mixed generations, and other "non-traditional families" do their best to adapt standard dwellings to their daily needs.

This chapter is entitled "Revolutions" because it demonstrates how houses have changed to accommodate new types of households, living patterns, and ideas about what a house can be. Several houses respond to demographic shifts. For example, with longer life spans and improved health, more aging homeowners are inclined to live on their own, in their own homes, as long as possible. Few are willing to give up their independence and privacy by moving into retirement communities or, as was once more common, in with their grown children. The latter scenario occurs less often today, in part because young families, faced with tighter real estate markets and fewer affordable options, are buying houses much later than previous generations were able to. Resurrecting the idea of the family compound might begin to make economic sense again in the context of the housing shortages we have seen in recent years.

Three of the following houses are multigenerational, with designs that acknowledge the varying needs of their diverse households. Steven Holl's Y-House in the Catskills is configured to accommodate the activities of a couple and their adult children. The Y plan derived from the desire to separate the sleeping quarters of the parents and children, each occupying different branches of the Y. Toshiko Mori's Cohen House in Osprey, Florida, goes one step further, with an entirely independent, freestanding addition to the main house, a classic by Paul Rudolph. The new quarters house the homeowners' three grown children, affording both generations freedom and privacy, as well as proximity to each other.

Daly, Genik's Valley Center House in the San Diego mountains is the primary residence of an eighty-four-year-old man who wanted the house also to serve the needs of his children and grandchildren on their long and frequent visits. The house's U-shaped plan responds to the household members' shared and individual activities, while its construction—most notably its movable walls—allows it easy transformation from a large house to a small house.

Just as the profile of the average household has shifted, so has how we use and regard our homes. Technological gadgets have been altering the workings and form of the domicile for ages: Modern plumbing brought the outhouse in; electrical appliances turned kitchens into efficiency centers; TVs, VCRs, and surround-sound stereo systems spawned media rooms; and, one of the most significant revolutions in recent years, the affordability of personal computers, fax machines, and modems has made home offices a standard feature of many homes, even for individuals who don't telecommute. The house is now much more than a family nest; it is also a place for growing a business, for earning a second degree, for home-shopping. Again, spatial flexibility is a key requirement. Homeowners increasingly value spaces that can be easily converted—into offices, guestrooms, gyms, nurseries, or whatever best happens to suit their needs at a particular moment.

Boston-based Kennedy & Violich's house in Western Massachusetts is the ultimate reflection of a blended, peripatetic lifestyle. Their clients wanted a variety of things, including a home office, gallery space, plus a lap pool and dance studio to help keep the empty-nesters healthy. The architects struggled to find a solution, for they were loathe to cram different functions into small, undesirable rooms. Their breakthrough came when they decided to put everything together, within a single volume. The homeowners did not have a problem with overlapping functions in one space, since they liked the seamlessness between the various aspects of their lives.

Remodels, rehabilitations, and additions can serve as an index of the degree to which our lives have changed and older houses no longer appropriately serve them. Commissioned to update a 1950s suburban ranch house, San Diego architecture firm Public responded with an act of preservation and practicality: They encased the old house in a two-story concrete box that added square footage overall, but more importantly, it permitted the old house to be entirely reconfigured. Most of its interior walls were knocked down, transforming its spaces essentially into airy lofts. Meanwhile, Philadelphia architect Wesley Wei was charged with the task of making an eighteenth-century farmhouse a twenty-first-century home for an intensely private bachelor. Located on the rural outskirts of Philadelphia, the result is a collage of old and new, a series of masking façades that conceal the loftlike spaces within. Essentially, the home is one vast art gallery.

Just as a home can now house anything within it, any structure is now capable of housing a home—a warehouse, a power station, a factory. The Los Angeles firm RoTO forged a home out of the abandoned machine shop of an electrical power station. As important as the technical ability to reclaim these types of spaces is our psychological ability to drive through an industrial district and call it home. Volatile real estate markets have forced developers and buyers to reform their attitudes about habitable territory. Moreover, as the economy continues its evolution toward service and information industries, different types of spaces and landscapes are becoming available, forcing new interpretations of unusual contexts. RoTO's Carlson-Reges House is a grand loft, continuing in the tradition that artists began decades ago, carving out live/work studios in abandoned postindustrial districts and, importantly, allowing its owners to live in an urban context that they found crucial to their creativity.

The advent of the loft will prove to be the most significant revolution in domestic space in the late twentieth century. The same feature that so appealed to artists—expansive, uninterrupted space—is perfectly suited to our increasingly casual lifestyles and predilection for flexibility. Formal rooms such as living rooms, even separate dining rooms to some degree, have become obsolete. The open loft is becoming mainstreamed, gradually absorbed into condominiums, apartments, and houses in the form of single, large, multipurpose rooms. The vocabulary of the domestic building is changing, if slowly.

Another lifestyle revolution that is having profound implications for domestic architecture is a growing emphasis on leisure. Beyond the home theaters and built-in gyms, indoor swimming pools and home art galleries, what about entire outbuildings devoted to whim and pleasure? In Fayetteville, Arkansas, architect Marlon Blackwell built a treehouse for grown-ups. While it can be looked on as a genuine folly, it also relieves some of the pressure from the main residence, providing a place for quiet retreat, entertainment, and children's recreation.

Contemporary life is more frenetic and fast, variable and unpredictable. There's so much more we seem to do at all hours and in all places—work, play, travel, lounge, shop, socialize, exercise, and so on. Space both accommodates and modulates our activities. The fact is, the imagery of the ideal house and building techniques—not to mention its economics (banks are reluctant to finance unconventional houses)—change half as fast as our lifestyles do. But the houses in this chapter indicate that these other factors will eventually catch up, too.

Steven Holl Architects
Y-House
Catskills, New York
1999

New York architect Steven Holl, known for subtle, luminous buildings such as the St. Ignatius Chapel at Seattle University and Helsinki's Kiasma Museum, created a 3,500-square-foot home in upstate New York for two generations of a single family, an Austrian couple and their grown children. Holl's initial design idea was so simple—and so pleasing to his clients—that his first sketch became the final built product, with few modifications. The architect envisioned a pair of rectangular volumes that split into a Y-shaped configuration (hence the name of the home, the Y-House) to house the two generations' joint daytime and separate nighttime activities. He placed stairs along the inside of the Y's legs to let the exteriors of the two wings focus outward to views of the Catskill Mountains.

One enters the house at the base of the Y (in reality, the house is more like a distorted V than a proper Y), where a primary staircase rises to generate circulation up, down, and diagonally through the home. One branch of the Y contains an open, informal kitchen and dining area that are shared by both the parents and children; the other wing contains a pair of bedrooms for the adult children, each with a private bath, and a shared enclosed porch. Upstairs, the master bedroom is placed above the kitchen wing, to maximize nighttime privacy between parents and children; an open, airy living room is located above the children's bedroom wing. Both ends of the Y open onto covered terraces facing the choicest views.

Even though there is careful separation of functions to ensure privacy, there are still connections between spaces. The living room and kitchen and dining area are connected visually across the central stair and a study off the master bedroom overlooks the double-height entry foyer. The actual bedroom areas, however, are secluded at opposite ends and on different floors of the house. This plan of overlapping spaces simultaneously creates privacy and generates communal activities within the same space.

The movement into the house and up through it, from the low entry into the soaring double-height spaces, echoes the way one approaches the site: A road winds up from thickly forested areas and gives way to an open plateau on the family's property, where the house sits. Its peculiar form and quirky pattern of randomly placed windows and doors is completely invented, a response to the family's needs and the home's surroundings. The color, however, comes from a more familiar source: the bright red of dairy barns that dot the local landscape.

Architect Steven Holl's Y-House, painted the same bright red as local dairy farms, rises from the rural landscape of the Catskill Mountains of New York State. Covered terraces on both levels of the split volume face the best views.

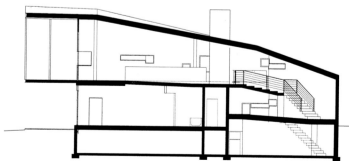

East-west section

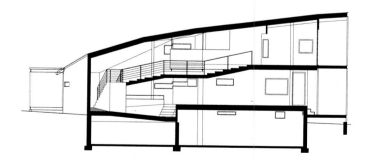

East-west section

The bedrooms
of two genera-
tions of the same
family are placed
on the second
floor of one wing
(facing page, at
left) and the
ground floor of
the other wing,
to maximize pri-
vacy. The house
tapers from a
single story at
the entrance
to two levels. The
seam between
the two wings of
the house (left)
reveals the
abstract window
pattern set
into the painted
cedar siding.

143
house
Revolutions Steven Holl Architects, Y-House

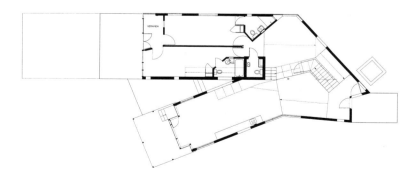

Ground-floor plan

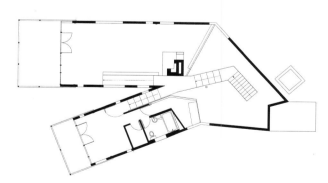

Second-floor plan

The front door opens directly onto the wooden staircase that winds along the two legs of the house's Y-shaped plan **(top left)**. To the left of the stair **(top right)** lies the kitchen and dining area, which opens onto an outdoor terrace; to the right is a foyer leading to a pair of ground-floor bedrooms for the younger generation of homeowners. At the top of the staircase is a built-in custom desk **(facing page)**, part of the second-floor master suite, overlooking the entry foyer below. The desk, along with all the home's cabinetry, was designed and built by New York-based FACE Design, longtime collaborators with architect Steven Holl.

In addition to joining living and bedroom spaces on two levels of the house, the staircase helps generate activity across different levels (above left). The master bedroom (above right) is located on the second level of one of the house's two wings, at the top of the Y-shaped stair (facing page, left). Windows behind the bed face views of the Catskill Mountains, while glass doors open onto a covered terrace. On the top floor of the opposite wing is the living room (facing page, right), also with a large window wall facing the mountains, where both generations of the family come together.

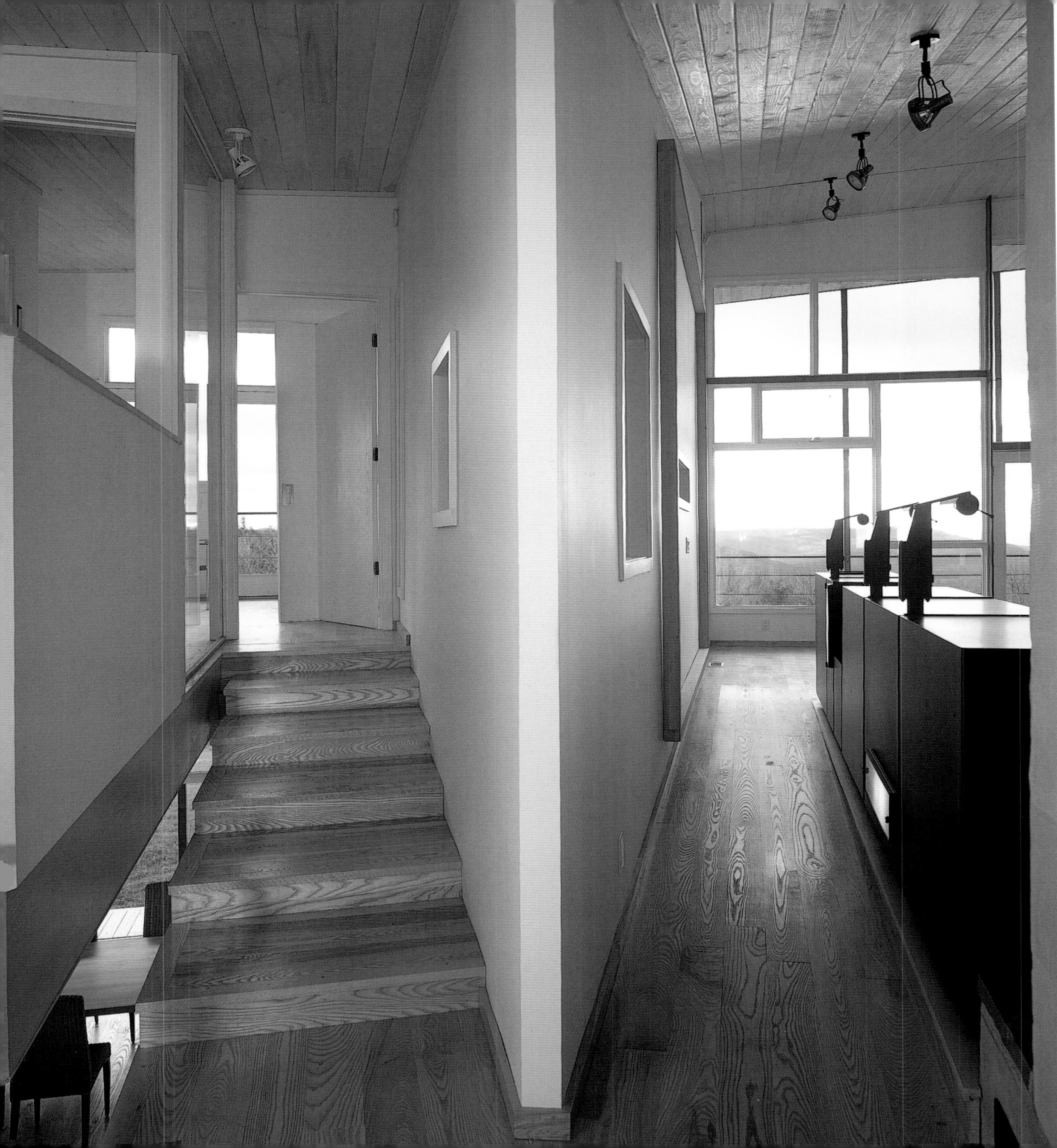

Valley Center House
San Diego, California
1999

In many cultures, the tradition of several generations living under the same roof is imbedded in the architecture. For instance, historically, in China, domestic compounds were organized to provide a degree of privacy to different branches of the extended family, as well as collective areas for sharing meals and recreational activities. It is more common today for people to live with only their immediate families, though perhaps they would think differently if there were more architectural alternatives that made living with parents and in-laws easier.

The Valley Center House serves the daily needs of an eighty-four-year-old retiree as well as the sporadic requirements of his children and grandchildren on their frequent and extended visits. The 2,850-square-foot house is a one-level (his only requirement was "no stairs"), angular U-shaped compound. It occupies the site of a suburban ranch house that burned in one of the Santa Barbara mountains' recent and seemingly regular brush fires.

The base of the U contains the kitchen, living and dining areas, and the two nearly identical wings are devoted to the bedrooms. They surround a paved courtyard and rectangular pool. The meeting point, both physically and socially, of the two wings is a 20-by-32-foot living room, an entirely glazed box, popped up higher than the wings with clerestories. The room faces west, with a clear view of the Pacific Ocean. On hot days, however, the room—in fact, the whole house—would be a sweltering greenhouse if it weren't for the motorized perforated-aluminum shell that architects Kevin Daly and Chris Genik devised. The screens are attached to aluminum tube frames, which, on the living room volume, lift like garage doors along horizontal I-beams supporting the roof. When rolled up, the screens act as shade canopies.

The two wings are screened with the same perforated aluminum, but their walls pivot like shutters, allowing varying degrees of light and shade. The screens serve not only to temper the weather, but to modulate the house according to how many people are using it. An entire wing can be sealed if no one is occupying it. Additionally, sliding opaque screens separate the bedrooms from the hallway, allowing them to be either open or private. With these sliding walls, the number of bedrooms can range from four to seven. The bedrooms themselves are spare; the house is more about the outdoors than in.

The house has a severe, almost inelegant appearance, with its bare concrete foundations and floors, exposed metal structure, and warehouselike demeanor. But its skeleton and skin are pragmatic in this hazard-prone terrain. The massive concrete fireplace in the living room serves as a seismic anchor for the house, while the metal shell provides a degree of fire protection. The house is an example of responsive, flexible architecture that adjusts according to heat, light, wind, and use.

Designed to meet the needs of an elderly man and his extended family, this house has a U-shaped plan that encloses a courtyard with a pool. At the base of the U is the glazed lofty living room and kitchen. Bedrooms line the two side wings. To allow different levels of enclosure and shade, the façades are equipped with perforated-aluminum screens that lift up and pivot. The screens on the living room volume roll up with the help of electric motors, sliding along cantilevering I-beams that frame the roof. When slid up, they act as brise-soleils or canopies.

The retractable screens are used on the front façade (above), as well as the courtyard-facing walls. The garage-door workings of the screens allow the building to be transformed into an open pavilion. The house has the basic, functional demeanor of an industrial shed or trailer, but its setting—the earthquake- and fire-prone San Diego mountains—demands rugged, high-performance solutions. The straightforward steel-and-glass structures sit on bare concrete floors.

Bedrooms are lined up, shotgun-style, along the two side wings and are fronted by pivoting aluminum screens that can be positioned to direct wind and light **(above left)**. The multigenerational family compound can be modified according to how many people happen to be using it.

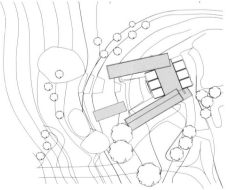

Site plan

When all the screens are closed, the house looks as plain as a shipping container **(above)**. But, capable of varying positions and movement—horizontal for the side wings, and vertical for the central family room—the screens give the house added dimensionality, while also modulating light, wind, use, and mood **(facing page)**.

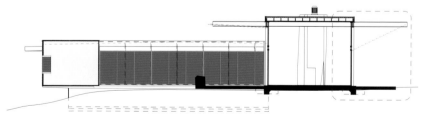

Section through living room and courtyard space, showing exterior wall of bedroom wing

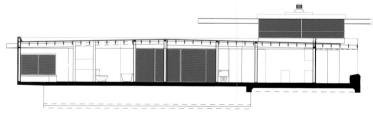

Section through entry and kitchen, showing interior wall

The two nearly identical side wings **(section drawings, above)** meet at the soaring, 20-by-32-foot living room, at the base of the house's U-shape plan. Essentially a glass box, the living room is organized around a massive concrete fireplace **(above left)**, which ties into the roof joists and serves as a seismic anchor. To one side of the fireplace is the kitchen **(above center)** and dining area, and to the other is a sitting room **(floorplan, facing page)**.

Ground-floor plan

The number of bedrooms in the house can vary from four to seven at any moment, necessitating only the push of the sliding walls that serve as doors to the bedrooms **(facing page and above)**. The rooms are warmly tinted but stripped-down simple, like the lodgings at a summer camp, employing Murphy beds and other built-in furniture.

Toshiko Mori Architect
Cohen House
Casey Key
Osprey, Florida
2000

New York architect Toshiko Mori was asked to design a guesthouse for a family home near Sarasota, Florida. The request, however, was more complex than it might sound: The primary house was a restored 1957 beach home designed by the legendary modern architect Paul Rudolph during his prolific building career in Sarasota in the 1950s. The Rudolph-designed house had a particular modern character, with spaces arranged to generate natural cross-ventilation and shaded but bright interiors intimately linked to the outdoors. Mori's new guesthouse had to more or less follow the size and footprint of an earlier, 3,000-square-foot structure that had been destroyed by a hurricane. To make matters more complicated, though, local hurricane codes had changed radically since the original house was built—forcing the architect to lift the living spaces safely above flood levels. And its owners, who had lived through the meticulous restoration of the original wooden Rudolph home, wanted this structure to be low maintenance. Finally, the guesthouse was to house the three grown children of the owners of the main house, requiring a delicate balance of privacy and proximity.

Mori responded to this complicated task list with elegant aplomb, taking inspiration from the original Rudolph house's cantilevered roofs and thin floor plan. She broke the guesthouse into two pavilions arranged in a T shape and lifted them a full story above the ground, on concrete columns. (An exterior weatherproof steel stair connects the two wings of the guesthouse.) Added benefits of being forced to lift the structure up on stilts are the feeling of being in a treehouse among a lush grove of live oaks, and improved views of the Gulf of Mexico on one side of the house and Little Sarasota Bay on the other.

Both legs of the T-shaped guesthouse are only one room wide, to allow cross-breezes that ventilate the house. One leg of the T contains a small bedroom and bathroom, an airy living and dining room, a kitchen, and a covered terrace. The other, shorter leg shelters a bedroom and bath and a smaller living room on one level and a second bedroom with a bath and a private terrace with outdoor shower on a second level upstairs.

The home's materials are basic and indeed low maintenance, as requested by its owners. The ceilings are sealed concrete; the walls painted concrete block; and the floors ground concrete in some areas and bamboo sheeting in others. There are large expanses of glass—a combination of clear, opaque, and patterned panels—shaded from the sun by steel louvers. Mori designed most of the furniture, including birch bookshelves, bathroom vanities, and a steel-and-plastic desk. When she did not (or could not) design furnishings, the architect picked cool, modern pieces that complement the sleek but simple surroundings.

Architect Toshiko Mori built a guesthouse for the grown children of the owners of a Paul Rudolph-designed house from the 1950s atop the existing foundations of a long-gone structure. The house had to be raised a full floor above the ground to meet Florida hurricane regulations that guard against flooding.

The guesthouse is a long, skinny box nestled among live oaks; it is kept intentionally slender to generate natural breezes through the house. Its skin is clad in concrete block and large windows shielded by stainless-steel louvers.

Revolutions Toshiko Mori Architect, Cohen House

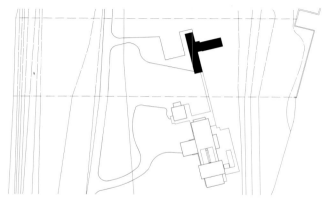

Site plan

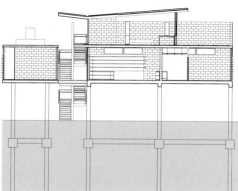

East-west section

The T-shaped guesthouse is composed of two pavilions joined by an exterior stainless-steel stair (facing page). The shorter end of the T has a second level, a butterfly-roofed volume containing a second bedroom and a terrace, which peeks out above the first floor. The longer stem of the T ends in a shaded outdoor terrace (left).

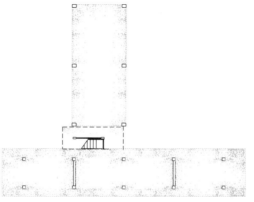

Garden-level plan

Second-floor plan

The guesthouse's interiors are minimal, with exposed concrete ceilings and floors, painted concrete block walls, and some areas of flooring made of bamboo, as in the living room of the shorter wing of the house **(facing page)**. The architect designed the birch shelving units in that living room. The guesthouse's other wing contains an airy living and dining area **(above)**, filled with cool, minimal furniture.

Thanks to floor-to-ceiling windows and glass doors, the water and lush vegetation are always visible from indoors, including the living room **(above)** and bedroom **(below)**. The exterior staircase outside the living room windows continues up to the second-floor bedroom and rooftop deck.

The exterior staircase outside the living room windows continues up to the second-floor bedroom and rooftop deck. The second-floor bedroom features a custom-designed desk made of stainless steel and plastic (left). Just outside is a roof deck with an outdoor shower.

Public Art and Architecture
Su Mei Yu House
La Jolla, California
2000

The ranch houses of the 1940s and 1950s—the great postwar building boom that spawned Levittowns and suburbia—have been much maligned in recent times. While it is true that these homes have done little to advance the state of architectural design, they have offered affordable homes for the middle class for more than half a century. And they represent a significant chunk of the available housing stock in much of suburban and semi-suburban America.

The young San Diego–based architecture firm Public recognized the inherent value of such homes, even though they did not relish their design. When a couple in nearby La Jolla asked them to add onto the 1950s ranch that they had lived in for almost twenty years—an original Sears & Roebuck kit house that the owners wanted to preserve—the architects responded with a practical solution that celebrated the vintage home, quirks and all. They designed a two-story concrete-box wrapper that encases the original avocado-green house as an artifact in a museum display case.

The addition provides 900 square feet of new space above the single-story, 1,250-square-foot original structure. The concrete-block addition extends beyond the footprint of the original house, so the architects left a two-foot gap between the new façade and the old walls and paved this in-between space in pebbles, suggesting that the exterior landscape has entered the home. This gap between new and old structures emphasizes the design's aggressively original concept of preserving—rather than demolishing or consuming—the old house.

The architects reconfigured the downstairs, removing doors and windows but leaving walls intact, into a living room, office, kitchen, and master bedroom within the existing shell. Upstairs, they added an airy library and gallery with an adjoining balcony focused on an ocean view, and a tiny bathroom; a staircase tucked within the zone between the new façade and the old façade joins the two levels. In the new library, the avocado-green walls of the old house peek up through the floor—once again, to reinforce the fact that the 1950s ranch has been preserved within a new shell.

Inside and out, the addition's materials are simple and affordable (the entire project cost $300,000). The thick concrete-block walls are speckled with black and gray pumice and given a satiny finish, to render them more exotic than standard-issue blocks. The rest of the addition is made of unpainted, exposed steel beams and wooden joists, and inexpensive metal-framed shopfront-style windows and doors. In the spaces of the original ranch, existing materials such as parquet floors were left as is. The architects planted shrubs between two layers of chain-link fencing along the home's entry façade, which they expect will overgrow the industrial fence and soften that elevation a bit. Though many homeowners might find Public's project too quirky for their tastes, it is a worthwhile investigation into how to adapt a ubiquitous building—the dreaded suburban ranch—into a livable, modern home.

Architect Public's strategy of preserving a 1950s ranch house within a new expansion is evident in the street façade, where a tiny, gabled portion of the original home peeks out from the concrete-block addition. The house sits upon a pedestal of black bricks and is screened from the street by shrubs that will eventually grow through and cover a chain-link fence. A tiny second-floor balcony overlooks the Pacific Ocean.

The house's backyard elevation **(facing page and above)** reveals new materials–concrete block, siding, and overhanging wooden roof beams–and the original redwood siding, painted avocado green. A terrace supported on large steel beams extends beyond the second-floor library and gallery.

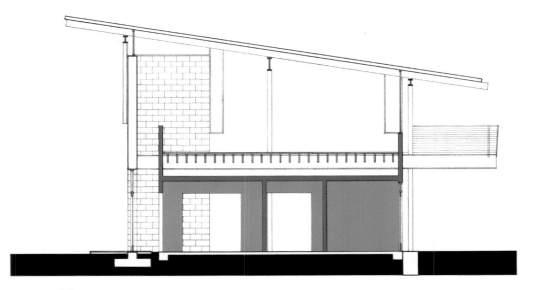

Section through library

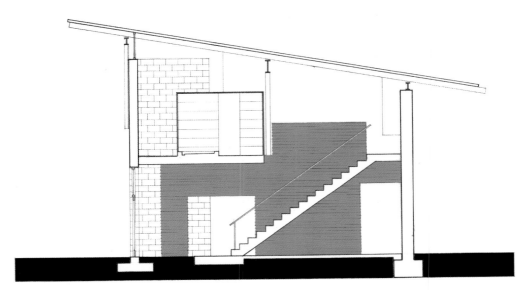

Section between inner and outer shell

The living room
is contained
within what was
the shell of the
original house,
preserved within
the concrete-
block walls of
the two-story
addition like a
museum artifact
**(facing page and
section drawings,
left).** Built-in
shelving allowed
the owners
to drag many of
their books,
which had not
fit in their older
home, out
of storage.

Revolutions Public Art and Architecture, Su Mei Yu House

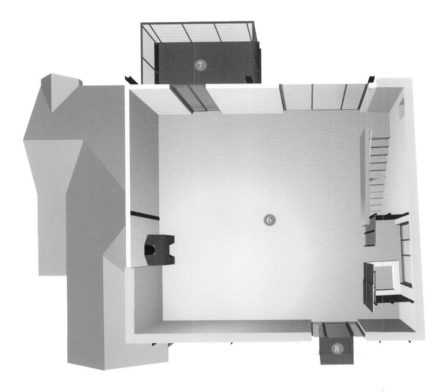

Second-floor plan

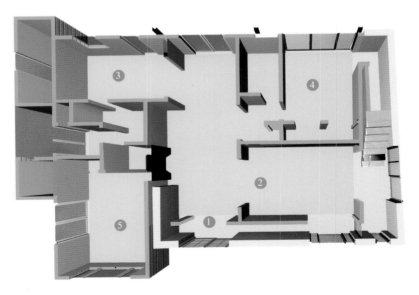

Ground-floor plan

Since the original structure is swallowed up within the larger addition, what were once exterior walls, painted bright avocado green, are now interior walls **(facing page)**. To emphasize the difference between the house's old and new parts, the architects left a narrow gap between the original and newly built walls and paved the space with gravel.

The new 900-square-foot library on the second floor is an airy, loftlike space perfect for one of the owners, an artist. A narrow window between two different walls captures a sliver view of a California palm tree **(above)**. The open area features a mix of hard-nosed materials, including steel beams, aluminum-framed windows, exposed wooden roof beams, concrete-block walls—and even an original wall that peeks up into the new space **(facing page)**.

Pennsylvania House
Media, Pennsylvania
2000

For a house in Media, Pennsylvania, architect Wesley Wei's primary challenge was to update a small eighteenth-century fieldstone farmhouse to suit the needs of its owner, a bachelor with a sophisticated art collection. The Philadelphia-based Wei admits that he was intimidated at the prospect of designing a home for not just a man with exacting taste but for the masterful creations of Francesco Clemente, Alberto Giacometti, Anselm Kiefer, George Baselitz, and Louise Nevelson. The client pushed him to design a house that would do more than serve his daily needs, and even more than simply display art. He wanted a house that would rival the masterpieces it would contain.

The result is a deft three-dimensional collage, with startling combinations of materials, forms, and periods. His interventions are as dramatic as they are functional. The original building, a 700-square-foot two-story pitched-roof box, had endured numerous clumsy additions in the past, which Wei eliminated entirely. His additions are distinctive volumes with independent architectural integrity that also manage to respect the identity of the old farmhouse. Corten steel, lead-coated copper, and western cedar clad the new parts of the building—materials that Wei felt carried as much visual weight as the old. Deployed monotonously, these materials also render the exterior façades inscrutable, which was crucial to the privacy-crazed homeowner.

Inside, it is obvious that the spaces have been organized and designed with specific artworks in mind. Just inside the entrance, a gallery space vaults eighteen feet upward, clearly tailored for a large painting by Kiefer. The kitchen, which spins off the original stone house like a satellite, is a narrow, compact galley—a departure from the spacious combination kitchen-living rooms seen in many contemporary houses, but utterly suited to the client, who rarely cooks or entertains.

This house is more art gallery than house, which explains why material treatments are kept simple and nondistracting. They might even be described as deliberately harsh: poured concrete walls, steel beams cutting through the old and new parts of the house, exposed sections of the original thick stone walls, and more. This hard-edged aesthetic echoes the look of contemporary art's natural habitat—warehouse-converted galleries and artists' studios.

Like these neutral art settings, the rooms in the house's new wing are reserved, subdued—all the better for focusing attention on the artwork. To deepen the house's sense of quiet, a channel of dark gray river stones imparts the living room with a Zenlike air. The new elements seem especially idiosyncratic in relation to the old stone and pine floors (salvaged from old barns) of the renovated old house. Just like good art, the house surprises, delights, and challenges the mind and the senses.

In a suburb of Philadelphia, in an area that has retained its rural character, this house transforms an eighteenth-century fieldstone farmhouse into a contemporary bachelor retreat and veritable art gallery. The rear of the house overlooks a koi pond. The main addition to the house **(left of the original stone house)** is glazed at the ground level, and clad in lead-coated copper on the second floor, concealing the master bedroom. The kitchen is an autonomous volume attached to the other side **(right)** of the farmhouse; its cedar siding emphasizes its independence and counterbalances the visual weight of the other exterior surfaces (stone, metal, and glass).

The front of the house **(above)** is reserved, fittingly, for the homeowner prizes his privacy. The architect deliberately chose new materials that would stand up to the old stone walls. The kitchen is a small, narrow volume that extends from the old farmhouse **(facing page)**. Clad in cedar planks, the room sits on a plinth of concrete blocks. The kitchen is set off from the main house and is diminutive, because the homeowner rarely cooks or entertains.

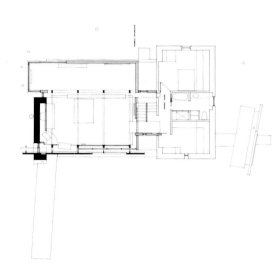

Second-floor plan

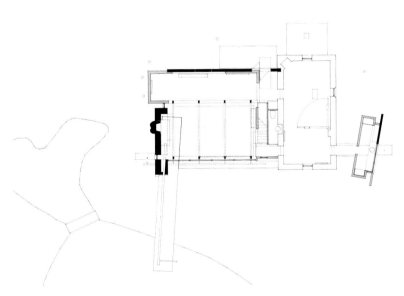

Ground-floor plan

The ground floor of the main addition is awash in sunlight, not only from the expansive sliding glass walls facing the back garden, but also from the exposed aluminum grate on the ceiling, which allows light from the bedroom above to filter through. The original stone house serves as a gallery space **(center of the ground-floor plan, below)**, as does the long rectangular space at the front of the house, adjoining the living room. The kitchen is detached from the main house **(to its right)**. The master bedroom floats above the living room **(the second-floor plan, above)**, which is supported by a steel-frame structure.

An eighteen-foot-high gallery space at the front of the house was designed to accommodate a large painting by Anselm Kiefer **(above)**. The floor of the addition is a step below that of the original stone house, to mark the transition from old to new **(facing page)**. The new part of the house is framed in exposed steel. A channel of river stones imparts the room a Zenlike calm.

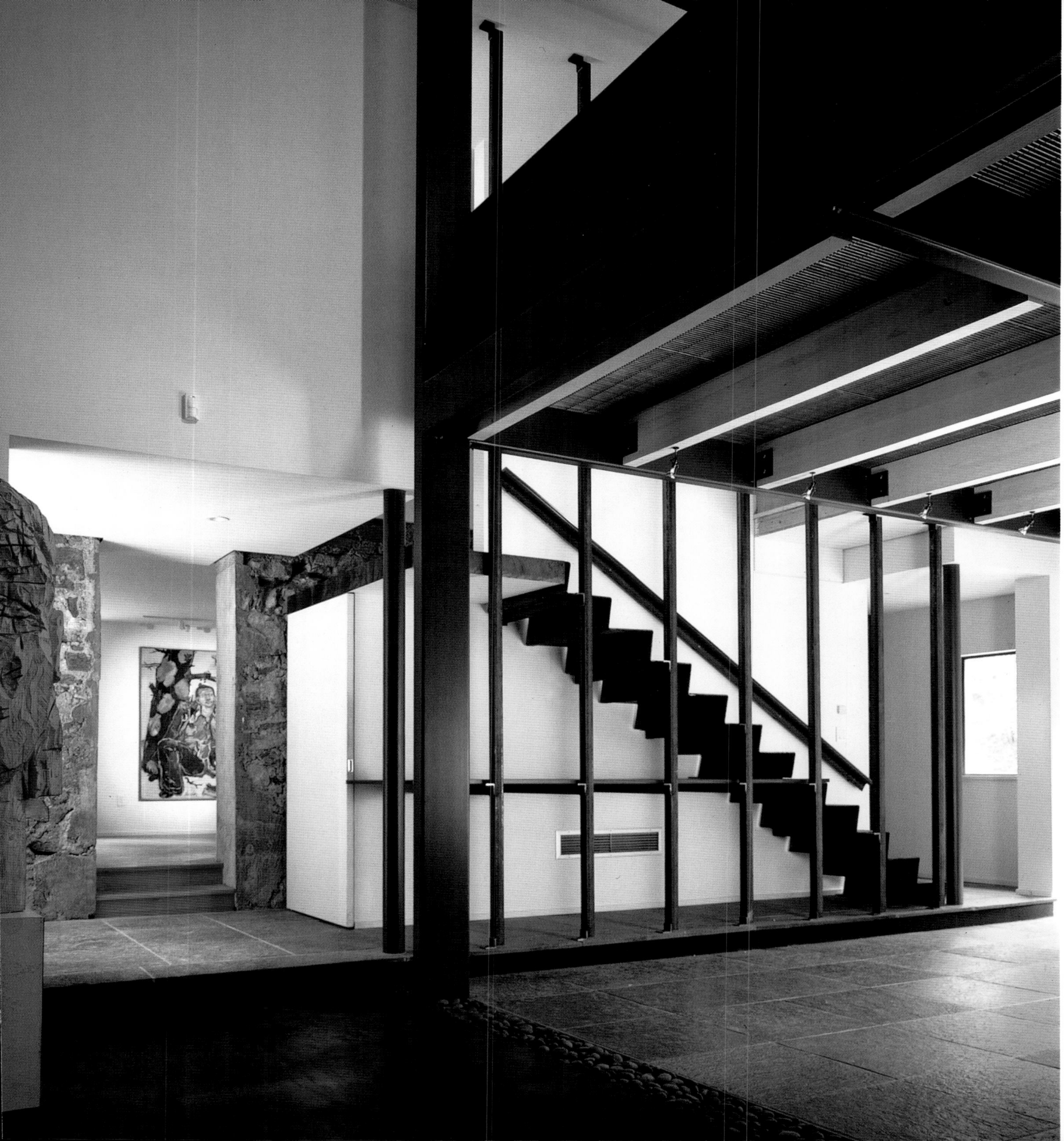

The architect left the places where the old and new house meets the exposed **(above)**, drawing power from the contrast of textures and time periods. The wall of the second-floor master bedroom curves outward, toward the rear pond **(facing page)**. It gives added dimension to the otherwise rectilinear room, where the steel-frame structure is continued from the ground floor below.

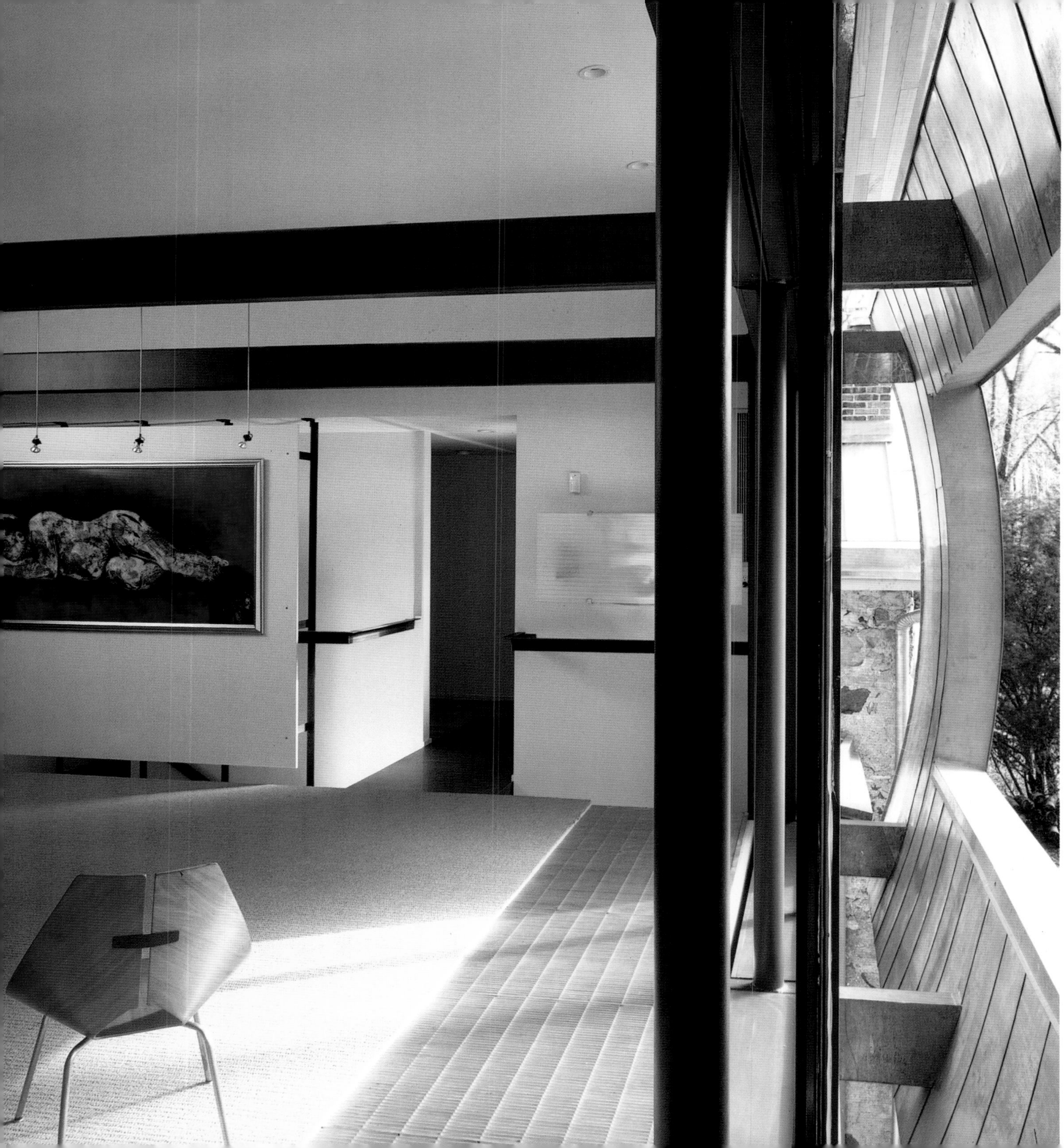

RoTO Architects
Carlson–Reges House
Los Angeles, California
1997

Transforming former industrial spaces into sophisti-cated dwellings has become common practice in America's down-towns. Loft living first took flight in New York City, where the endless search for square footage and affordable shelter helped transform old factories and warehouses into flexible, open apart-ments and workspaces. Of course, the artists who pioneered the trend in formerly nonresidential Manhattan neighborhoods such as Soho and the Meatpacking District have now been priced out of these areas—a trend that is continuing in places such as Chicago, Seattle, and San Francisco. In these cities, demands for new living spaces and a wealth of underused industrial buildings also helped the loft approach flourish.

Even residents of Los Angeles have started looking at their grittier neighborhoods as fertile ground for clever conversions. The Los Angeles–based architecture firm RoTO, the brainchild of for-mer Morphosis partner Michael Rotondi and partner Clark Stevens, took the idea of turning industrial artifacts into homes to a new level. RoTO designed a house for an art collector and a demolition contrac-tor that takes as its starting cue the abandoned machine shop of Los Angeles's first electrical power station, located next to railyards adjoining downtown. While most loft commissions are little more than interiors jobs within a stripped-down shell, RoTO's project transforms the inside of a machine shop's neoclassical container and then breaks out far beyond the box.

The massive wooden entry door opens onto a staircase that leads to the living areas, which are located on the top two floors of the three-story house. There is also a double-height studio for the wife, an artist, that is a light-filled, whitewashed space crowned by an exposed steel structure that supports the upper reaches of the house. An unexpected treat in such a gritty industrial setting is the private garden located off the studio.

The entry stair winds up to a kitchen on the second floor, which also contains a soaring living and dining area (overlooking the studio below) that opens onto an outdoor deck cantilevered beyond the house. Adjoining the deck is one of the home's quirkier ele-ments: a lap pool made from a slice of a rusty industrial gas tank. The third floor is an entirely new level atop the original electrical building, created from cast-off trusses and beams that the architects scavenged in a steel-girder depot next door to the house. This penthouse level, an angular shell of smooth and rusty metal, contains a large master suite with a huge dressing area and another private outdoor deck. From this level, the residents enjoy sweeping vistas of Los Angeles, from the towers of downtown to the surrounding mountains.

What is most inventive about the house is that the architects foraged through the industrial depots that surround the site to find the materials they needed to expand the original structure. They left the historic shell largely intact, removing doors and windows only so they could extend the house above and beyond it, and crafted new spaces from old beams and trusses. Though it is very rough-and-tumble, the loft is also very clever and dramatic—and environmentally friendly, given the recycled materials it incorporates.

The Carlson-Reges House, designed by Los Angeles architects RoTO, takes the idea of loft living to new heights: It is adapted from a vintage electrical power station and crafted, in part, from industrial cast-offs found in depots near the site.

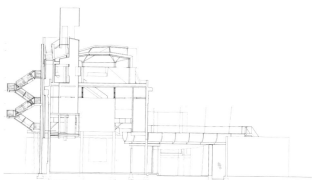

Transverse section east-west

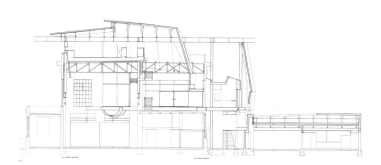

Longitudinal section north-south

The house fills the neoclassical shell of the power station's old machine shop, part of a gritty industrial area on the edge of downtown Los Angeles **(facing page)**. The master bedroom is housed inside a metal box extending beyond the roof of the original vintage building **(far left)**. Canted walls of industrial materials shield a new staircase on the exterior of the home **(left)**.

South elevation

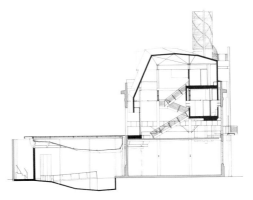

Transverse section west-east

A garden behind the house is a welcome oasis of green in this gritty neighborhood **(above)**. Hanging over the garden is a lap pool crafted from an unexpected industrial remnant: a slice of a fuel tank that cantilevers beyond the second-floor living room **(facing page)**.

The ground floor contains a double-height art studio and gallery, filled with natural light **(facing page)**. Visible above is the solid end of the fuel tank-cum-lap pool, which backs into the interior. The living and dining area is a soaring two-story space on the second floor animated by exposed structure and angled walls in subtle colors **(left)**. A staircase behind the fireplace leads to the master suite and dressing area above.

Third-floor plan

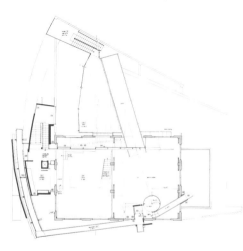

Second-floor plan

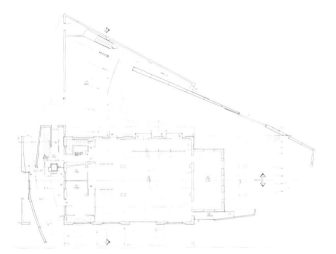

Ground-floor plan

The underside of the rusty lap pool extends above the lush, quiet garden **(above)**. The steel structure of the house remains exposed throughout, giving the house a tough industrial quality **(facing page)**.

Kennedy & Violich Architecture
Residence and Gallery
Western Massachusetts
1999

Ask anyone and they will tell you that the boundaries of their daily lives are getting blurrier by the day. More Americans than ever before are working from home and from the road, eliminating the distinctions between the dreaded office and the domestic haven. And although people spend more time laboring at home, it is still the place where they relax after the cell phone stops ringing and the computer is turned off. In short, the home is becoming many things at once: office and sanctuary and place of recreation and entertainment.

Boston architects Sheila Kennedy and Frano Violich gave physical form to this confluence of daily activities in their 3,300-square-foot addition to a suburban Boston house. The clients, active empty-nesters whose lives required more space instead of less, requested a lap pool, a dance studio, a home office for the husband, and space indoors and out for their growing art collection. Rather than cramming separate functions into separate rooms, the architects decided to throw out convention and combine and overlap disparate functions into a single volume.

The most obvious repercussion of their design strategy is the 48-foot long, mosaic-tiled swimming pool, which plows right through the center of the space—and cantilevers beyond the exterior walls—with all the subtlety of a submarine crashing through a house. To one side of the pool, which is enclosed by sliding glass panels and disinfected with ozone to keep the house from smelling like chlorine, is the workout space; on the other is the loftlike living area. The dining area is located at the short end of the long rectangular pool, close to the original home, which still contains the couple's kitchen, study, and three bedrooms. Although there is plenty of daylight thanks to light wells and abundant windows, the illumination is carefully controlled to avoid damaging the art collection and to provide comfortable light levels for viewing pieces by Andy Warhol, Claes Oldenburg, and Christo, among others.

On the second floor of the addition, directly above the exercise studio, is a spacious office accessed by a staircase in the living room that bridges the interior pool. As it crosses over the pool, the single sheet of maple plywood composing the bridge floor forks in two directions. Part of the wooden surface descends into the office as a ramp; another continues level with the bridge, to become a built-in desk overlooking the wooded surroundings through large expanses of glass. This gesture is a perfect metaphor for the entire home—a single element that does double duty, like the spaces that reflect and accommodate increasingly complex lives. With its easy flowing spaces, the house creates new, unexpected connections between art, work, leisure, and exercise.

This addition to a suburban home in Western Massachusetts, designed by Boston-based Kennedy & Violich Architecture, contains a host of new work and leisure functions for an empty-nester couple. Large clerestory windows wrapping the boxy addition provide ample daylight inside.

Site plan

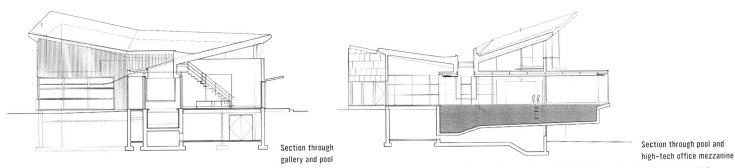

Section through
gallery and pool

Section through pool and
high-tech office mezzanine

The new structure, clad in zinc shingles, has its own entrance at the rear of the property **(facing page, above left)**. The smaller glass-enclosed block cantilevered beyond the building **(above left and facing page, above right)** contains an unexpected interior lap pool. The landscaped grounds behind the addition provide space for the owners' sculpture collection. The steeply angled roof atop the addition **(above right)** echoes the gabled roof of the existing home, visible to the right of the addition in the above left photograph.

The unorthodox centerpiece of the addition is an interior swimming pool **(facing page)**, which plows right through the heart of the home. Enclosed in sliding glass panels, the pool also serves to divide the home's central space into distinct areas: living room, exercise and dance studio, and a home office. The room is left open and airy, allowing the homeowners to showcase their collection of contemporary art.

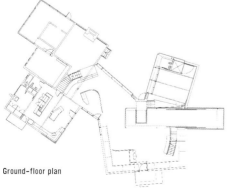

Ground-floor plan

Second-floor plan

The dance studio is tucked behind the lap pool **(facing page, above left)**. A staircase leading up to the second-floor office area bridges the pool **(facing page, above right)**. The wooden ramp and stairs that access the office splits to become a continuous work surface along the wall of windows **(above left and right)**.

The owners' art collection is illuminated by carefully controlled daylight that enters through strategically placed clerestory windows and light wells **(above)**. A glass wall set into the steel frame enclosing the lap pool creates a transparent barrier between the pool and the loftlike living area. Sliding glass doors enclosing the long sides of the pool **(facing page)** are adjustable, to create varying degrees of openness and acoustical privacy.

Marlon Blackwell
Keenan Tower House
Fayetteville, Arkansas
2000

The tower house that architect Marlon Blackwell designed for a young couple in Fayetteville, Arkansas, caused a bit of controversy in this small town in the Ozark Mountains. The 82-foot-tall retreat is similar in concept and structure to a fire tower, water tower, or grain silo. But as a house above the trees, it proved unconventional for local townspeople, who tried to stop its construction. Blackwell and his clients won the battle, and the young family is now enjoying its privileged panorama high above the hickory and oak forests. The design pays homage to the client's vivid childhood memories of a tree-house built by his grandfather, and also calls to mind commonplace industrial towers, as well as lighthouses, crows' nests, and other buildings of fairy tale and fancy.

Though the tower house is aggressively unorthodox, it is actually a simple steel-framed tower structure with a miniature loft on top, which is accessed by an open stair extending the full height of the tower. Visitors step through a steel-framed door at the ground level, enter a small, sheltered courtyard paved in local river and creek stones, and start climbing the five stories up to the living areas. The tower is wrapped in an irregular pattern of wooden slats and wide metal planks that create dappled shadows and provide guests with changing vistas of the home's 57-acre site as they wind their way upstairs.

Once inside the 560-square-foot living area, visitors are treated to wide-open views through the wall-to-wall windows wrapping all four sides of the tower. Inside are two floors of enclosed living areas: a foyer, bathroom, and kitchenette on one level; and a living and sleeping space one floor up. The interiors feature floors and walls of locally milled white oak.

Above the living area is an open-air deck, which Blackwell calls the "skycourt," accessed through a fold-down stair similar to an attic stair. A built-in table folds down from the western wall of the "skycourt" for impromptu picnics on the deck. Vistas from this rooftop entertaining area are framed through large openings in the slatted-wood walls that create postcard-perfect vignettes of the Ozark landscape—and of the open sky above.

Who says a guesthouse can't also be a treehouse? Architect Marlon Blackwell designed this guesthouse in a tower for a young family in Fayetteville, Arkansas, which recalls the area's industrial towers and grain silos.

The tower is clad in a combination of wooden slats and metal planks **(facing page)**. At night, lights behind the wood slats reveal the steel structure enclosing the staircase that winds up to the living spaces at the top of the tower **(left)**. The living and sleeping areas are wrapped in a continuous band of windows.

Revolutions Marlon Blackwell, Keenan Tower House

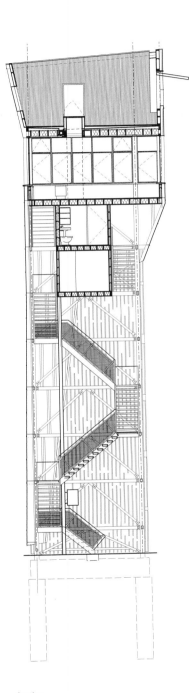

Section

The journey up the tower begins with a fairy-tale-like doorway at the base **(facing page)**, which leads to a small courtyard **(center)**. Views of the wooded landscape unfold through the slatted wood skin as visitors wind up five flights of stairs **(above left and below left)**.

Revolutions Marlon Blackwell, Keenan Tower House

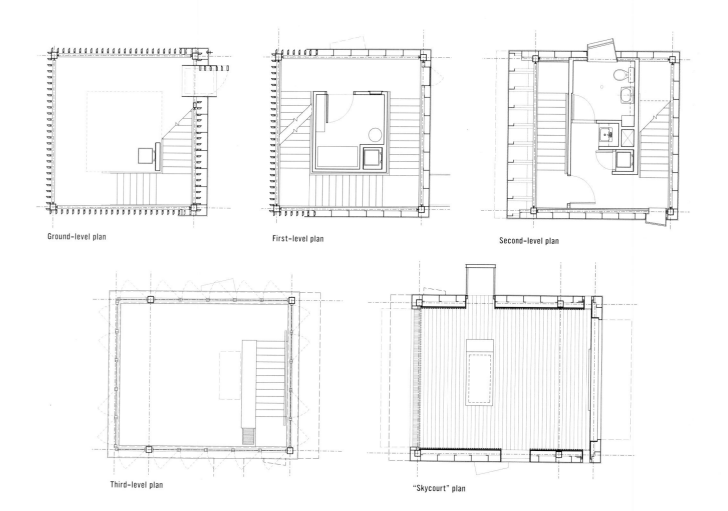

Ground-level plan

First-level plan

Second-level plan

Third-level plan

"Skycourt" plan

At the end of the journey up the tower is the sparsely furnished living and sleeping area **(facing page)** wrapped in a full band of operable windows that open onto endless panoramas of the landscape. Beneath the living space is a small kitchenette and bath. A hatch in the ceiling conceals a pull-down staircase that leads to a roof deck.

Behind the walls of the rooftop perch is an open-air deck, where guests at barbeques and picnics can survey the landscape through cut-out openings in the walls **(above)**. Seen from a distance, peering up above the trees **(facing page)**, the unconventional approach of the tower house makes perfect sense—to gain views and an adventurous spirit impossible to create on the ground.

Credits

Marlon Blackwell Architect

357 North Washington Avenue
Fayetteville, AR 72701
T. (501) 582-5634
F. (501) 575-7099

Keenan Tower House, Fayetteville, Arkansas

PROJECT PRINCIPAL: Marlon Blackwell

ENGINEER: Joseph Looney & Associates (structural)

CONSULTANT: Harness Roofing (metal siding)

CONTRACTORS: Razorback Ironworks, Pizzini, Don Lourie

PHOTOGRAPHY: ©Timothy Hursley

Wendell Burnette Architects

9830 North 17th Street
Phoenix, AZ 85020
T. (602) 395-1091
F. (602) 395-0839

Schall House, Phoenix, Arizona

PROJECT PRINCIPAL: Wendell Burnette

ENGINEERS: Rudow + Berry, Inc. (structural); Otterbein
Engineering (mechanical); C.A. Energy Designs (electrical);
Castro-Fleet (civil)

LANDSCAPE DESIGNER: Debra Burnette Landscape

GENERAL CONTRACTOR: Baywest Construction Management, Inc.

PHOTOGRAPHY: ©Timothy Hursley

Daly, Genik

1558 Tenth Street
Santa Monica, CA 90401
T. (310) 656-3180
F. (310) 656-3183

Valley Center House, San Diego, California

PROJECT PRINCIPALS: Kevin Daly, Chris Genik

ENGINEER: Armando Paez (structural)

CONSULTANT: Leif Johnson (architectural metal and canopy engineering)

GENERAL CONTRACTOR: Robert Lackey Construction

PHOTOGRAPHY: ©Undine Prohl

Fougeron Architecture

3537 21st Street
San Francisco, CA 94114
T. (415) 641-5744
F. (415) 282-6434

440 House, Palo Alto, California

PROJECT PRINCIPALS: Anne Fougeron, Russell Sherman

ENGINEER: Endres Ware Consulting Engineers (structural)

LANDSCAPE ARCHITECT: Topher Delaney

GENERAL CONTRACTOR: Young & Burton

PHOTOGRAPHY: ©Richard Barnes

Steven Holl Architects

450 West 31st Street, 11th Floor
New York, NY 10001
T. (212) 629-7262
F. (212) 629-7312
http://www.stevenholl.com

Y-House, Catskills, New York

PROJECT PRINCIPALS: Steven Holl, Erik F. Langdalen

ENGINEER: Robert Silman Associations (structural)

GENERAL CONTRACTOR: Dick Dougherty

PHOTOGRAPHY: ©Paul Warchol

Rick Joy Architect

400 South Rubio Avenue
Tucson, AZ 85701
T. (520) 624-1442
F. (520) 624-1442

Palmer-Rose House, Tucson, Arizona

PROJECT PRINCIPAL: Rick Joy
ENGINEERS: Southwest Structural Engineers (structural); Roy T. Otterbein (mechanical)
CONSULTANT: Rammed Earth Solar Homes
LANDSCAPE ARCHITECT: Michael Boucher Landscape Architect
GENERAL CONTRACTOR: Rick Joy
PHOTOGRAPHY: ©Wayne Fuji, ©Timothy Hursley (p. 34)

Tyler House, Tubac, Arizona

PROJECT PRINCIPALS: Rick Joy, Andy Tinucci
ENGINEER: Southwest (structural); Otterbein (mechanical, plumbing)
LANDSCAPE ARCHITECT: M. Boucher
GENERAL CONTRACTOR: Rick Joy
PHOTOGRAPHY: ©Jeff Goldberg / ESTO

Alberto Kalach

Atlanta 143
Col. Nochebuena Mexico, 03720, D.F.
T: (52) 5611-1771
F. (52) 5611-5044

Casa Negro, Contadero, Mexico City

PROJECT PRINCIPALS: Daniel Alvarez, Alberto Kalach
ENGINEER: Guillermo Tena (structural)
LANDSCAPE ARCHITECT: Tonatiuh Martínez
GENERAL CONTRACTOR: Daniel Alvarez
PHOTOGRAPHY: © Martirene Alcantara (pp. 103, 104, 108), ©Paul Czitrom (pp. 101, 106, 109), ©Luis Gordoa (pp. 102–103, 105)

GGG House, Chapultepec, Mexico City, Mexico

PROJECT PRINCIPAL: Alberto Kalach
ENGINEER: Enrique Martinez Romero (structural); Rafael Lopez (electrical)
LANDSCAPE DESIGNER: Tonatiuh Martínez
GENERAL CONTRACTOR: Miguel Cornejo
PHOTOGRAPHY: ©Jeff Goldberg/ESTO, Undine Prohl (p. 61-center photos)

Kennedy & Violich Architects

160 North Washington Street, Studio 814
Boston, MA 02114
T. (617) 367 3784
F. (617) 367 3727
http://www.kvarch.net

House For Contemporary Art, Western Massachusetts

PROJECT PRINCIPALS: Sheila Kennedy, Frano Violich, Markus Froehlin
ENGINEERS: Sarkis Zerounian and Associates (structural); Ibrahim & Ibrahim Engineers (mechanical)
GENERAL CONTRACTOR: Kistler & Knapp Builders, Inc.
PHOTOGRAPHY: ©Undine Prohl, ©Bruce Martin (pp. 201, 203-right, 204, 205)

Lake/Flato Architects

311 3rd Street, Suite 200
San Antonio, TX 78205
T. (210) 227-3335
F. (210) 224-9515
http://www.lakeflato.com

Bartlit House, Castle Pines, Colorado

PROJECT PRINCIPALS: David Lake, Karla Greer
ENGINEER: Datum Engineering, Tom Taylor (structural); M-E Engineers, Inc. (mechanical)
LANDSCAPE ARCHITECT: Kings Creek Landscaping, Inc.
INTERIOR DESIGN: Bruce Gregga Interiors
LIGHTING DESIGNERS: Fisher, Marantz, Stone Architectural Lighting
GENERAL CONTRACTOR: Beck & Associates
PHOTOGRAPHY: ©Paul Hester/Hester & Hardaway

Brian MacKay-Lyons Architecture Urban Design

2042 Maynard Street
Halifax, Nova Scotia B3K 4K2, Canada
T. (902) 429-1867
F. (902) 429-6276
http://www.bmlaud.ca

House #22, Halifax, Nova Scotia

PROJECT PRINCIPALS: Brian MacKay-Lyons

ENGINEER: D. J. Campbell Comeau Engineering (structural)

GENERAL CONTRACTOR: Andrew Watts

PHOTOGRAPHY: ©Undine Prohl

Miller/Hull Partnership

911 Western Avenue, Suite 220
Seattle, WA 98104
T. (206) 682-6837
F. (206) 682-5692
http://www.millerhull.com

Michaels–Sisson House, Mercer Island, Washington

PROJECT PRINCIPALS: Robert Hull, Amy E. DeDominicis

ENGINEER: Dayle Houk (structural)

CONSULTANT: Quantum Windows (vertical-lift window)

GENERAL CONTRACTOR: Jeff Davis Construction

PHOTOGRAPHY: ©James Housel, ©Art Grice (pp. 124–126)

Toshiko Mori Architect

145 Hudson Street
New York, NY 10013
T. (212) 274-8687
F. (212) 274-9043

Cohen House, Casey Key, Osprey, Florida

PROJECT PRINCIPALS: Toshiko Mori, Pedro Reis, Timothy Butler

ENGINEER: Stirling and Wilbur Engineering Group (structural)

LANDSCAPE ARCHITECT: Quennell Rothschild & Partners

GENERAL CONTRACTOR: Michael K. Walker and Associates

PHOTOGRAPHY: ©Paul Warchol

Barton Myers Associates

1025 Westwood Boulevard
Los Angeles, CA 90024
T. (310) 208-2227
F. (310) 208-2207

Myers House, Montecito, California

PROJECT PRINCIPALS: Barton Myers, Clint Wallace, Don Mills, Cal Smith

ENGINEERS: Epstein/Francis & Associates (structural), Ove Arup & Partners (mechanical), Barton Myers Associates (electrical); Norman H. Caldwell (civil); Pacific Materials Laboratory (soils)

CONSULTANT: Finish Hardware Technology (hardware)

LANDSCAPE ARCHITECTS: D. G. Richardson, Victoria Myers

GENERAL CONTRACTOR: R. H. Coffin

PHOTOGRAPHY: ©Grant Mudford

Public Art and Architecture

4441 Park Boulevard
San Diego, CA 92116
T. (619) 682-4083
F. (619) 682-4084
http://www.publicdigital.com

Su Mei Yu House, La Jolla, California

PROJECT PRINCIPALS: James Brown, James Gates, Freddie Croce

ENGINEER: Flores, Lund, and Mobayed (structural)

CONSULTANT: Brummitt Energy Associates (energy)

LANDSCAPE ARCHITECT: Aeria

GENERAL CONTRACTOR: Public

PHOTOGRAPHY: ©David Hewitt and Anne Garrison

Mack Scogin Merrill Elam Architects

75 J.W. Dobbs Avenue NE
Atlanta, GA 30303
T. (404) 525-6869
F. (404) 525-7061

Nomentana House, Lovell, Maine

PROJECT PRINCIPALS: Merrill Elam, Mack Scogin, Lloyd Bray

ENGINEER: Uzon and Case Engineers (structural)

INTERIOR DESIGN: Margaret Nomentana, ASID

LANDSCAPE ARCHITECTS: Michael van Valkenburgh Aassociates

GENERAL CONTRACTORS: Mark Conforte, Conforte Builders

PHOTOGRAPHY: ©Timothy Hursley

Shim+Sutcliffe Architects

441 Queen Street E
Toronto, Ontario M5A 1T5, Canada
T. (416) 368-3892
F. (416) 368-9468

Muskoka Boathouse, Lake Muskoka, Ontario, Canada
PROJECT PRINCIPALS: Brigitte Shim, Howard Sucliffe
ENGINEERS: Atkins + Van Groll Engineering (structural); Toews Systems
Design (mechanical)
GENERAL CONTRACTOR: Judges Contracting
PHOTOGRAPHY: ©James Dow

RoTO Architects
600 Moulton Avenue, #405
Los Angeles, CA 90031
T. (323) 226-1112
F. (323) 226-1105
http://www.rotoark.com
Carlson-Reges House, Los Angeles, California
PROJECT PRINCIPALS: Michael Rotondi, Clark Stevens
ENGINEER: Peter S. Higgins and Associates (structural)
CONSULTANTS: Donald T. Griggs (steel fabrication); Richard Reyes; Arkkit-
forms (furniture)
GENERAL CONTRACTOR: Richard Carlson
PHOTOGRAPHY: ©Assassi Productions, ©Benny Chan/Fotoworks (p. 193),
©Tim Street-Porter (p. 198)

Wesley Wei Architects
100 North 3rd Street, 2nd Floor
Philadelphia, PA 19106
T. (215) 593-8118
Pennsylvania House, Media, Pennsylvania
PROJECT PRINCIPALS: Wesley Wei, Stephen Mileto
INTERIOR DESIGN: Maria Izak Nevelson Interior Design
GENERAL CONTRACTOR: Phillip Johnson Construction, Inc.
PHOTOGRAPHY: ©Catherine Bogert

Acknowledgments

This book was initiated by former Universe architecture editor Richard Olsen, whom we must thank for getting us off on the right foot. We are deeply grateful to our graphic designer, Claudia Brandenburg, who always knew exactly what to do and did it with great professionalism and an even greater sense of humor.

Thanks to all the architects, without whose work this book would not be possible. Thanks, too, to the many photographers who contributed to this book. Erica Stoller at ESTO, Linda Achard at Timothy Hursley/The Arkansas Office, and Richard Barnes deserve special mention for their endless helpfulness and generosity.

We are grateful to our editor, Terence Maikels, for his care and patience; to Sarah Amelar at *Architectural Record* for sharing a shoot as well as her ideas; and to Linda O'Keefe and Arlene Hirst at *Metropolitan Home* for their helpful suggestions. Liane Lefaivre and Richard Ingersoll have been a constant and much appreciated source of inspiration. And lastly, we can't thank our families and friends enough for their support and encouragement.